CW00428293

MASTER TH

Fifty CEOs tea

secrets of time management

Pat Brans' compelling book shows you how to get more done faster than ever before. More importantly, you'll learn to do things of greater value.

Brian Tracy
Author, Time Power and Eat That Frog

History's greatest leaders understood the importance of time management. *Master the Moment* by Pat Brans is the best book I have ever read on the subject. Exhaustively researched, skillfully conveyed, and insightful in its applications, this book should be required reading for anyone who aspires to be an effective leader.

Donald T. Phillips
Author, Lincoln On Leadership

Pat Brans has grilled dozens of top achievers for their secrets. This book is a lively, entertaining, and inspiring compilation of their wisdom. Every reader will find some useful tips for a better, happier, more successful life.

Dr Roy F. Baumeister
Author, Is There Anything Good About Men?

This book is strewn with pearls of practical wisdom on the art of time management gleaned from fifty chief executives. It is a great guide to becoming a better time manager, especially for those in more senior leadership positions. Lively, stimulating and fun.

John Adair
Author, Effective Leadership Development

Master the Moment is the most complete book on time management I've seen. It explains underlying ideas, it provides useful techniques, and it even includes a well-founded and practical approach to changing habits.

Brad Stock
President of the American Chamber of Commerce in Lyon, France

Pat Brans gives us a tool for self-discovery, to find what we do best and where we fall short with Father Time. Looking through the eyes of the world's highest achievers, this book will guide you to see yourself at the head of the boardroom (or of your family) and provide you with tips on how to live a fuller life.

Roby Chavez
Reporter, Fox Television Inc., Washington, DC

Pat Brans' style, anecdotal and practical, makes *Master the Moment* a true pleasure to read. Beyond entertaining and insightful, it is full of stories that are both useful and inspirational. The examples demonstrate that the people who accomplish remarkable things in business are not those with the most 'natural talent', but rather those who are most willing to evolve and improve. Time management is a learned skill, and we can all learn from this book.

John Sadowsky
Author and leadership coach

BCS, The Chartered Institute for IT

Our mission as BCS, The Chartered Institute for IT, is to enable the information society. We promote wider social and economic progress through the advancement of information technology science and practice. We bring together industry, academics, practitioners and government to share knowledge, promote new thinking, inform the design of new curricula, shape public policy and inform the public.

Our vision is to be a world-class organisation for IT. Our 70,000 strong membership includes practitioners, businesses, academics and students in the UK and internationally. We deliver a range of professional development tools for practitioners and employees. A leading IT qualification body, we offer a range of widely recognised qualifications.

Further Information

BCS The Chartered Institute for IT
First Floor, Block D
North Star House, North Star Avenue
Swindon, SN2 1FA, United Kingdom
T +44 (0) 1793 417 424
F +44 (0) 1793 417 444
www.bcs.org/contactus

MASTER THE MOMENT
Fifty CEOs teach you the
secrets of time management

Pat Brans

Published by British Informatics Society Limited (BISL), a wholly owned subsidiary of BCS The Chartered Institute for IT First Floor, Block D, North Star House, North Star Avenue, Swindon, SN2 1FA, UK.
www.bcs.org

ISBN 978-1-906124-73-1

British Cataloguing in Publication Data.
A CIP catalogue record for this book is available at the British Library.

Disclaimer:
The views expressed in this book are of the author(s) and do not necessarily reflect the views of BCS or BISL except where explicitly stated as such. Although every care has been taken by the authors and BISL in the preparation of the publication, no warranty is given by the authors or BISL as publisher as to the accuracy or completeness of the information contained within it and neither the authors nor BISL shall be responsible or liable for any loss or damage whatsoever arising by virtue of such information or any instructions or advice contained within this publication or by any of the aforementioned.

Typeset by Lapiz Digital Services Chennai, India.
Printed at CPI Antony Rowe, Chippenham, UK.

for Louise

CONTENTS

LIST OF FIGURES AND TABLES

AUTHOR

Pat Brans provides corporate training on time management and personal effectiveness. He is also visiting professor at the Grenoble Graduate School of Business (GGSB).

Brans has held senior positions with three large organisations (Computer Sciences Corporation, Hewlett-Packard, and Sybase). Most of his corporate experience focused on applying technology to enhance workforce effectiveness. Now he takes productivity to another level by unveiling the secrets of high achievers.

ACKNOWLEDGEMENTS

Writing a book is a lot of work. You can't easily do it alone; nor would you want to. Getting feedback and fresh ideas from many knowledgeable people is an essential part of the process.

For this book I got a lot of help. First, I'd like to thank all the CEOs featured in this work. The book couldn't exist without them.

For encouraging me to develop Master The Moment as a time management methodology, I thank Peter Wildhorn, Tom Brans, Emily Huschen, Agnes Cadoux-Dubus, Jerry Cave, and Chin-Hsia Chang.

For helping me set up my business to provide training and seminars on time management, I thank the following people: Brigitte Treguer, Elisabeth Mantello, Nathalie Gary, Mikael Lund, and Anne-Laure Bernardin.

For making introductions to some of the CEOs featured in this book, I'm indebted to Chris Elliot, Miles Faust, William Hydrick, Charles Monteiro, Anna Brans, Henry Brans, Gloria Rall, Jennifer Hew, and Barbara Wolf.

For helping make this a better book, I also thank the following people: Danielle Chiotti, John Biguenet, Patrick Mulvanny, Richard Zimmer, John Chancellor, Christina Rebuffet-Broadus, April Buchanan, and Trudi Penkler.

ABBREVIATIONS

CEO	Chief Executive Officer
SDT	Self Determination Theory

PREFACE

Do you have time to read this book? If so, you stand to gain a lot of excellent ideas from some of the world's most effective people. If, on the other hand, you don't think you have the time, maybe you should stop whatever you're doing and have a look. In these pages lie important ideas on how to get more out of your day – how to use your most precious resource more wisely.

Have you ever wondered why some people go through life frustrated, whereas others are able to accomplish most of what they set out to do without breaking a sweat? After all, each of us has the same number of hours per day. In fact, time might be the only resource that's evenly distributed.

Yet, somehow, some people get so much more done. It's almost as if they perceived time differently. To them, they are moving along at a comfortable speed, getting things done with time left for family and personal hobbies. To a bystander they are zipping past. The purpose of this book is to find out what makes these people different – and to uncover a few of the secrets of some of the world's highest achievers. You can put these ideas to work for yourself and Master The Moment.

The tips you'll find here come from chief executive officers (CEOs) with aggregate responsibility for over a trillion dollars, and millions of people. They took time out of their busy schedules to talk to me about time management and personal effectiveness. Take the time to listen to what they have to say. I'm sure you'll find this a worthwhile investment.

PART I:
THE RIGHT MINDSET

1 HIGH ACHIEVERS

'There is a very important point in life that we ought to maximise. It is this moment. This moment is now gone.'

That's what Frank Stewart told me when I asked for advice on time management. He should know a few things about getting the most out of every instant. After all, he grew his company, Stewart Enterprises, from a family business with 15 people in the suburbs of New Orleans to a publicly traded multinational. At its peak his company had more than 6000 employees, and subsidiaries as far away as New Zealand.

Frank went on to explain: 'My profession is quite unusual. I'm in the death care industry, where we sell products and services for funerals, burials, and memorials. This means I'm in a business in which there is no way you can ignore the fact that time does run out. I see it all around me. Every one of us will die one day. This is without question.'

'There are so many things I want to do,' he said. 'I easily fill the day. There just isn't enough time to do it all. It's because I have so much to do – and because of my profession – that I am acutely aware of the limited nature of time. I think about time management constantly.'[1]

Frank went on to share some of his secrets on maximising the moment. We'll cover them throughout the book. But first let me tell you where I'm coming from.

---

[1] Exclusive discussion with Frank Stewart, April 2008.

I started out my professional life as a software engineer and gradually moved into the business side of the technology industry. I spent the last 10 years of my time in high tech finding ways of making people more productive through the use of mobile technology.

It was satisfying to see how salespeople and technicians could get more done thanks to the latest gadgets. Still, there was something missing. Certainly mobile phones and laptops are tools that help people do things faster. But they don't account for the difference between people who accomplish most of what they want and those who go through life frustrated.

To shed some light on this I decided to talk to a group of people who are very good at using their time: CEOs. After all, these people are responsible for running large organisations. They have to manage a lot of money and a lot of people. To do their jobs and attend to their personal lives they have to be on top of their game.

I know most people aren't trying to become CEOs. But top executives can teach us a lot about the human dynamics that apply to virtually any job. And let's not limit this discussion to work. These same concepts are just as appropriate to your personal life.

For this book I spoke to 50 CEOs in a variety of industries and in different countries. I read the autobiographies of several other chief executives. To top it off I researched what psychologists and other experts have to say about motivation and personal effectiveness. In these pages I hope to share with you all of their great tips.

Let's start out by taking a look at how much some people are able to get done with their time.

WHAT SOME PEOPLE GET DONE

Some people have a tremendous capacity to get things done. Take for example John Dane III, an Olympic athlete at the age of 58. In the summer of 2008 he competed at the Olympic games in Beijing as part of the US sailing team. He is also CEO of Trinity Yachts, a company that builds custom-made luxury yachts and sells them for tens of millions of dollars around the world. On top of that he's a minority partner in a second company that manufactures and sells navy patrol boats. John does things he's passionate about. And he doesn't give up easily. He first tried out for the Olympics in 1968 and came in second. He has tried several times since, and finally, 40 years later, he made it. In the meantime he completed a PhD in engineering, started a company, and raised a family.[2]

Another person who gets a lot done is Lucas Skoczkowski. Lucas exercises an hour and a half a day, he reads 50 books a year, he speaks English, Polish, and French, and a little Swedish. He's currently learning Chinese and Arabic. While he's not doing all that or spending time with his family, Lucas runs Redknee, a fast-growing high-tech company that sells equipment for mobile phone networks. By the way, Lucas is only 35 years old. He has a good sense of humour, and he doesn't give me the impression that he's working himself to the point of exhaustion. On the other hand, he's very selective about where he applies his effort.[3]

Then there's John Jamar, a marathon runner and a triathlete. He happens to be the CEO of CCI Systems, a fast-growing cable network solution provider. What's more, he is on the boards of directors of several non-profit organisations. John still has time to spend with his family and is actively involved in the lives of his two sons. He also finds the time to hunt. John says being in shape has helped him tremendously. When you're in great shape you sleep well at night and you get through your days with a whole lot more energy.[4]

Certainly these three people are doing something right. They run sizeable companies, yet still they manage to have hobbies, raise families, and get much more exercise than the average person does.

And what about people who overcome catastrophes and still come out way ahead? They may be even better examples of good time management.

---

[2] Exclusive discussion with John Dane III, March 2008.
[3] Exclusive discussion with Lucas Skoczkowski, April 2008.
[4] Exclusive discussion with John Jamar, March 2008.

Take for example Dan Packer, whose wife died of a rare liver disease, leaving him alone to raise their two children. He went through tough times as a single father, but in spite of the hardship he rose to the rank of general manager of a nuclear power plant. Later he became CEO of Entergy New Orleans, a Fortune 500 energy company. An African-American growing up in segregated Alabama, Dan surely picked up some tools to help him to deal with tough situations. More recently, his can-do attitude was demonstrated when he brought Entergy out of bankruptcy following Hurricane Katrina.[5]

What about Gertrude Boyle (Boyle with Tymchuk 2007), a German Jew who escaped Nazi Germany in the nick of time? She emigrated to the United States at the age of 13 with her family. When she was 47 her husband died of a heart attack, leaving her alone with three children and a small company to run. Her husband had just taken out a loan for $150,000 with the house as collateral. Having been a stay-at-home mom up to that point, she knew nothing about running a business. But the situation was forced upon her. She had to dig deep to muster the courage to rise to the occasion. Success didn't come quickly for her, either. In the first few years she nearly ran the company into the ground. Creditors were pushing hard for her to sell it and get out of the business. But Gert learned from her mistakes and turned things around. In 2008 her company, Columbia Sportswear, reported revenue of $1.3 billion!

I asked Gert how she managed to get through all of that and come out smelling like a fresh bouquet of roses. She told me she didn't consider her situation that difficult. At first I thought she was making it up, but I soon realised that what she had done was to choose her perspective on catastrophic events. As difficult as her crisis would appear to most people, to others who are dealt an even less favourable hand it would have seemed relatively easy. She chose to take the second perspective: that her situation was relatively easy. She also chose where to focus her efforts. She went on to say that she does not waste time and energy dwelling on the past. Instead she thinks about what it is best to do now and in

---

[5] Exclusive discussion with Dan Packer, October 2008.

the future. To me Gert's life is an excellent demonstration of the power of managing your attitude, a topic we'll cover in detail.[6]

Gertrude Boyle escaped Nazi Germany as a young teenager. Years later, when she was 47, her husband died of a heart attack, leaving her alone with two children and a small clothing business in dire straits. A homemaker with no experience in business, she turned Columbia Sportswear into a billion-dollar global operation.

Does Gert think her situation was particularly difficult? Actually, she doesn't. Her attitude is to focus on the present and the future. Put your effort into those things you can change. Make things better today – and if you can't do that, make them better tomorrow.

Let's turn our attention to some of the CEOs of very large companies – let's say, companies with over $5 billion in revenue. How do they manage their time? Are they completely consumed by their jobs? I don't think so. Consider the following examples indicating that many of them have full lives outside their work.

Jean-Pascal Tricoire runs Schneider Electric, a $20 billion multinational – among the 500 largest companies in the world. He is also an avid kayaker and adventure seeker. Jean-Pascal is also married and has three children. Work is certainly not the only thing in his life.

Most people have heard of Larry Ellison, who runs Oracle Corporation, one of the biggest software vendors in the world. Throughout his adult life he has been an passionate practitioner of several sports. These include body surfing, mountain biking, sailing, and aerobatics in decommissioned fighter planes.

And just about everybody on the planet knows about Richard Branson, who runs several companies in a variety of industries under the Virgin brand. His Virgin Group makes over $25 billion

---

[6] Exclusive discussion with Gertrude Boyle, August 2008.

a year and employs over 55,000 people. Yet he still finds the time to engage in death-defying sports such as ballooning around the world.

NATURAL ABILITY VERSUS GOOD TIME MANAGEMENT

Look around at people you know. Surely you've noticed that some get a lot more done than others do. What sets these people apart is not an overabundance of innate ability. Nature did not endow them with more talent than many of the people around them have. But don't take my word for this. Listen to what some of the CEOs featured in this book have revealed about themselves.

Sandra Kurtzig struggled with mathematics in school. She overcame her difficulties by working on them, and later she majored in mathematics in college. She went on to start and run ASK Computer Systems, one of the first large software companies in the world. And she did it at a time when few women were working.

Her observation on why some people are more successful than others is: 'They are the ones who can recover from bad ideas quickly and effectively, who are persistent and can parlay their mistakes into success.'

Sandra Kurtzig has always been a slow reader. When she was in elementary school her parents were told she had an average IQ. In junior high school teachers said she wasn't bright enough to be in the advanced mathematics class. That's not to suggest that she didn't have some natural ability. She certainly did. But I think it's safe to say she didn't stand out as a genius at school. In any case, what brought her further than most kids with far more native ability were her determined efforts at self improvement. Sandra identified her weaknesses and found more efficient ways of learning the material that didn't come easily to her. She went on to get a university degree in mathematics. A few years later she started a software company, ASK Computer Systems, that she developed into one of the first major software companies in the world. She did this while raising a family. And she did it in the 1970s when fewer women worked outside the home. In fact, some men even openly stated they were hesitant to do business with her because of her gender. (Kurtzig with Parker 1994)

Then there's Sam Walton, who started Walmart and made it into one of the world's largest companies. He worked hard and was highly competitive, but there is nothing to indicate that he was born with an extra dose of talent. In fact, in reference to his education he said: 'I wasn't what you'd call a gifted student, but I worked hard and made the honor roll.' His attitude, and his determination constantly to do better, made the difference. Throughout his life he set goals and worked towards achieving them. (Walton with Huey 1992) David Glass, former CEO of Walmart, said this about his company's founder: 'Two things about Sam Walton distinguish him from everybody I know. First, he gets up every day bound and determined to improve something. Second, he is less afraid of being wrong than anyone I've ever known. And once he sees he's wrong, he just shakes it off and heads in another direction.'

The same goes for Ray Kroc, who made McDonald's into the company it is today. He might have been a talented pianist (he started his professional career as a pianist in the speakeasies of the 1920s). But there's no evidence to indicate that he was born a genius. Unsatisfied with his wages playing piano in bars, he then went on to selling paper cups. Then he sold multi-mixers, which were used to make several milkshakes at once. Among his biggest customers were the McDonald brothers, who kept several multi-mixers operating at once in their hamburger restaurant in San Bernadino, California.

Ray Kroc wanted to multiply this success by creating similar restaurants in other parts of the country. The idea was that the more McDonald's restaurants there were in operation, the more multi-mixers Mr Kroc would sell. So, with the agreement of the McDonald brothers, at the age of 52, Ray Kroc began to franchise McDonald's restaurants. This franchise business ultimately became the McDonald's corporation – and you can put it all down to tenacity. Mr Kroc made a lot of mistakes along the way. He stayed in debt for a long time. But, as everybody knows, he went on to run one of the most successful businesses ever. There is no indication that he had any unusual talent other than persistence and an ability to learn from his mistakes. (Kroc with Anderson 1977)

Now, going back to Richard Branson – the billionaire just about everybody on the planet has heard of – you might be surprised to learn that he is dyslexic. In school he was at the bottom of the class in every subject. His learning disability followed him into adulthood. Mr Branson says one of the things that was embarrassing for him was that, although he was running all sorts of companies around Europe, he couldn't understand the difference between gross revenue and net profit. It wasn't until he turned 50 and somebody drew a picture for him, visually displaying the difference between gross and net, that he finally got it! (Branson 2007)

Early in his career Lee Iacocca was shy and stilted. Through focused effort he overcame these handicaps and developed into such a good salesman that he rose to the rank of CEO of Ford Motors. Later on he was chief executive of Chrysler.

Don't get the idea that successful people are relying on natural ability. In the vast majority of cases they had to work at it and they had to overcome a lot of bad habits.

Let's not forget about Lee Iacocca, who says of his first experience in sales: 'Some people think that good salesmen are born and not made. But I had no natural talent. Most of my colleagues were a lot more relaxed and outgoing than I was. For the first year or two I was theoretical and stilted. Eventually I got some experience under my belt and started to improve. Once I had mastered the facts, I worked on how to present them. Before long, people started listening to me.'

Is this a surprising thing to hear from the man who became such a good salesman that he rose through the ranks of Ford Motors to become CEO? Mr Iacocca also says he was bashful and awkward in the early days of his career. Needless to say, he managed to find a way of overcoming that. (Iacocca with Novak 1984)

When I asked him about natural talent versus good time management, Lucas Skoczkowski insisted that most of the people around him are smarter than he is. The CEO of Redknee thinks he needs to carefully listen to what they have to say, because they usually have all the good ideas.

Lucas must be on the right track. After all, why would the CEO be the smartest or most talented person in the company? Anybody who's successful at leading an organisation knows that you only get ahead if you aren't afraid to hire people who are smarter than you. Taking this idea to its logical conclusion, famous advertiser David Ogilvy once said – in his own politically incorrect way: 'If each of us hires people smaller than we are, we shall become a company of dwarfs. But if each of us hires people bigger than we are, we shall become a company of giants.'[7]

Reflecting on how they built The Home Depot into one of the most successful companies of our time, cofounders Bernie Marcus and Arthur Blank say something along the same lines: 'One of our greatest accomplishments is hiring a cadre of people who are smarter than we are and who will one day run this business without us – even better than we did – and not miss a beat.' (Marcus and Blank 1999)

So it seems that people who get a lot done aren't necessarily the most talented. What about those who **are** the most talented? Well, if you're like me you probably know loads of brilliant underachievers – people who, despite an abundance of natural ability, spend their lives wallowing in frustration. Talent is important, but it's not the most critical factor in getting what you want.

What really sets high achievers apart is that they spend time thinking of ways of becoming more effective. They are **meta thinkers** – that is, they think about how they think and act, with the intention of making improvements. They apply their efforts where they can

---

[7] Exclusive discussion with Lucas Skoczkowski, April 2008.

make a difference, and recognise where there's nothing they can do to produce a change. Through introspection and careful use of their most precious resource, time, they are able to make things happen.

The good news is that anybody can do this if they're willing to put effort into it. The trouble is that most people don't.

Ray Titus, the CEO of United Franchise Group, told me: 'One thing that surprises me is there are a lot of people who don't do anything to improve their time management skills. They don't go to a seminar; they don't read a book on the subject. That's very unfortunate, because you can improve time management in almost every aspect of your life.'[8]

We've just covered a few of the powerful insights I gained from talking to CEOs. At this point you would certainly be justified in asking whether these ideas are supported by something more scientific. Did I base what I'm telling you only on my extensive conversations with top executives? Or can I back up what they told me with the results of other studies – with something researchers have come up with independently?

The answer is: I can. Scientists do support these ideas. And they have further insights to share.

Psychology researcher Carol Dweck (2006) has spent the last 30 years of her working life studying what motivates people and what elevates them to peak performance. She and other cognitive psychologists have found that there is a clear distinction between people who set performance-oriented goals versus those who set learning-oriented goals. The former group tends to do things to prove their current abilities. When they reach a goal, they view the achievement as validation of talent; but when they fail to reach a goal, they view the failure as a condemnation of their abilities. By contrast, those who set learning-oriented goals think they can build up skills over time to achieve increasingly challenging goals. For learning-oriented people, winning or losing is not a statement of their self-worth.

---

[8] Exclusive discussion with Ray Titus, July 2008.

TIP #1

Think of any given task as something you can work towards and master by learning, rather than something that tests your innate abilities.

Dweck and colleagues have found that those people who are performance oriented and who also perceive their competence to be low go through life feeling helpless. On the other hand, people who are learning oriented set more challenging goals and work towards them without fear of being shamed by intermediate failure. In fact, for these people any failure along the way is viewed as a learning experience. Because their ego is not tied to success or failure, they are more effective.

This might be shocking news with regard to the group of people featured in this book: CEOs. I know there is a stereotype of the chief executive officer with an ego the size of a planet. These are the bosses whose *raison d'être* seems to be stepping on the toes of those around them and proving they're genetically superior. Certainly it is true in some cases, but the most successful are those whose self-esteem is strong enough not to have to tie success or failure to personal worth. These are the people who accept challenging goals and then put their time to the best possible use in achieving those goals. They can relax in working towards what they want, because their self-image is never at stake.

Perhaps Lucas Skoczkowski puts it best: 'The less you have of something, the more you have to make conscious decisions on how you are going to use it. Time is your most limited resource. You had better get selective in how you use yours.'

Lucas goes on to say: 'CEOs may be ahead of the game, not because they are smarter but because they have identified the challenge of time management and they find ways to get better at it. The limited nature of time is an obstacle standing in their way. The path that leads them to discover the challenge is highly individual; and so is the set of tools they come up with to get beyond the obstacle. Hopefully, the tips in this book will serve as a catalyst to a large audience to allow them to spot the ways in which finite time poses a problem in their lives – and to find ways of maximising their use of their time.'[9]

Well put. Now let's zoom in on some of the ideas high achievers come up with.

EXERCISES

Before going on to the next chapter, try doing these exercises. They should be revealing. Be honest with yourself – after all, you're the only one who will look at your answers.

i   Make a list of some of the tasks you have worked on in the recent past – either in the context of work or in your private life – that you considered important, but that you either didn't bring to completion or completed later than you thought you should have.

    a   Next to each task, note the reasons why you didn't complete it. For example, did you get distracted? Did you lose interest?

    b   Now, next to each of the tasks, write down what completing it was going to mean to you. Was it a way of showing off or revealing your talent? Was it something that you thought people might laugh at if it wasn't perfect? **The answers to these questions are likely to explain what you put down during the 'a' part of this exercise.**

ii   Make a list of important tasks you are working on now. For each task, if you don't like the feeling you have about it, see what you can do to rethink your attitude. Challenge your assumptions. Can you view it as something that doesn't fundamentally change the way you and others see you?

---

[9] Exclusive discussion with Lucas Skoczkowski, April 2008.

iii Make a list of the separate roles you play in your life – for example, a family member, a member of a club, a friend, a hobbyist, or a professional. Note those areas where you think you're spending too much time and those where you aren't spending enough.

iv Do you feel you spend an appropriate amount of time thinking about time management? Some people think about it too much, others not enough. What about you?

v List the things you would like to get out of this book.

2 POWERFUL NOTIONS

We'll begin by taking a survey of some strategies with high impact. The CEOs featured in this book put these ideas to use in their own lives. Apply your efforts along these same lines, and you too will get more out of your time.

DOING THE RIGHT THINGS VERSUS DOING THINGS RIGHT

Thierry Grange is head of one of the world's top business schools, based in Grenoble, France.[1] Before taking that post, he started a company that sold motorcycles based on his own design. A larger motorcycle manufacturer then bought his company. In discussing time management with me, Thierry said that one key ingredient of overall effectiveness is 'the economic value of what you do'. If you sell potatoes you are going to work hard and not make so much money. If, on the other hand, you sell diamonds, you don't have to work as much, but you make much more money. The economic value of what you do has to do with the business you're in, but also with your position in the value chain within that business.[2]

How true this is. There are people who work really hard on an assembly line. And there are other people who work less hard thinking of ways of making production more efficient. The people in the first group put in more effort, and the work environment isn't as pleasant. While it may not be fair, the fact is that the person who sits in an office thinking of how to make an assembly line more efficient has a bigger impact.

---

[1] http://rankings.ft.com/businessschoolrankings/masters-in-management
[2] Exclusive discussion with Thierry Grange, April 2008.

Dr Gordon 'Nick' Mueller is President and CEO of the National World War II Museum in the USA. He is a serial entrepreneur who also happens to be a history professor. So starting and growing the museum to what it is today has been right up his alley.

Nick doesn't think he's very good at making use of every hour. However, he makes up for it by choosing the right things to do.[3]

It certainly is good to know how to do things right. But you get a far better payback when you know how to choose the right things to do. A less extreme comparison is where you choose something worthy of your efforts, but it's not the **most** worthwhile activity. You would be extraordinarily lucky if you always chose the very best thing to do. After all, you rarely have all the information needed to make such a perfect decision. The best you can do is make the best choice possible with what you know. By simply making a conscious effort to choose the best thing to do, you will see improvement. To take that still further, look for ways of getting better at the whole process of making such choices.

The simple lesson is this: before starting something, think about whether it's the best use of your time and energy. Then think about the best way of accomplishing it. Then do it. When you're finished, take a little time to think through how you can improve your initial judgement in selecting the right thing to do.

The most productive people in the world know this, and practise it so often that it becomes habit. They know that **doing the right things** is far more important then **doing things right**. They are acutely aware of their limitations, and they know that the best they can do is to choose where to apply their effort. Once they make that decision, they maximise the force they apply towards the goal.

In your personal life, as well as your professional life, be selective. Make sure you spend most of your time doing the things that are most important to you and that get you closer to where you want to be.

---

[3] Exclusive discussion with Gordon Mueller, April 2009.

ALIGNING YOURSELF WITH NATURAL LAWS

If you drop a hammer you know exactly what it's going to do: it's going to hit the ground. That's a law of physics – we just can't get around it. Sure, we are able to get hundreds of people off the ground and fly them to the other side of the planet. But that's not because we've defied the laws of physics. It's because we have made use of other forces – that of lift, in this case. We can be sure that if a wing or some other essential component of an aeroplane drops off, the plane will fall just as the hammer does.

Just as there are laws of physics, there are natural laws governing how human beings behave. We may not understand them all, but that certainly doesn't prevent them from existing. Unfortunately people don't come with a manual, so we have to figure things out ourselves. The most successful people make it a lifelong endeavour to tune in to human nature and make it work in their favour. They know they can't defy natural laws, so they don't try. Instead they strive to align themselves as best they can.

It's worthwhile reading up on the latest psychology research. I will cover some of that throughout this book. But most of what you need to know will come to you through trying to understand your-self and paying attention to other people. Try your best to put yourself in the other person's shoes.

You should also align yourself with natural laws governing your physical being. You need a certain amount of sleep, you need to eat right, you need exercise, and you need fun and satisfaction to stay motivated. Some people are under the mistaken belief that they get more done by staying up all night. This might work when you are faced with an emergency and left with no alterna-tive, but you'll have to pay back your sleep debt at some point. In the meantime, while you are sleep deprived, you won't be at your best.

Similarly, how you eat makes a difference in your energy levels throughout the day. If you eat heavy meals your body uses up a lot of energy to digest them, and this leaves relatively little for use elsewhere. Your body needs exercise to get the blood flowing and keep your muscles in shape.

Now let's consider natural laws underlying self-motivation. Our nature is such that we aren't able to get much done over extended periods of time if we don't get some kind of satisfaction out of the activity. If you like what you're doing, you stand a good chance of performing well; conversely, if you don't like what you're doing, you probably won't see many positive results.

Also remember that you have biorhythms – both physical and emotional. For example, if you're like 90 per cent of the people in the world, at certain times during the day you have more physical energy than at other times. Or your mood at certain times of the day is such that you're better able to deal with stressful situations. You might ask yourself, for example: are you a morning person or a night person? Biorhythms vary from person to person. The important thing is to tune in to your own.

Let's not forget about the natural laws governing how you deal with other people. Always remember that people have feelings and they have a will of their own. They are not machines that can be manipulated to do what you want. You can try coercion in its various forms. But in most cases, you wind up humiliating the other person. And he or she will either get upset with you overtly, or turn the anger inward. The net result is that people who are forced to comply will not give you their best in the long run.

> While he's not running one of the top ranked business schools in the world – the Ecole Supérieur de Management, based in Grenoble, France – Thierry Grange can be spotted zipping around the French Alps on his 1977 Ducati racing motorcycle.
>
> 'Don't try to fight natural laws,' he says. 'Align your mission with the world around you.'[4]

Aligning yourself with natural laws means understanding how you reason and then correcting for bias as required. We often hear the terms 'inductive' and its opposite, 'deductive', reasoning.

---

[4] Exclusive discussion with Thierry Grange, April 2008.

Inductive reasoning works **into** the theory. Deductive reasoning works **out of** the theory. Another way to put it is that inductive reasoning is what you do when you make observations and use them to build a theory. Deductive reasoning is when you use an existing theory or premise to explain an observation, to support a point, or to make a prediction.

We get pieces of data and we automatically construct a theory about how they were produced. It's quite unacceptable to us to have data with no theory to explain it. So we turn the data around and around in our heads until we come up with a model. Once we have a theory or model, we use it to make assumptions about new observations and to predict what's going to happen next. We may even ignore further data that contradicts our model.

From the standpoint of personal effectiveness, you have to remember that when you develop a theory of the world your own biases play a big role in shaping that model. When you settle on an understanding, you should never assume it's perfect. Challenge your assumptions. Be prepared to rethink your views if they don't seem to be in line with reality. Don't hesitate to come up with a new theory when the facts indicate that your current one no longer holds water.

Remember that personal bias comes from innate abilities and preferences in combination with past experiences. Your innate leanings and past experiences together give rise to emotion, which skews your perception of reality. Emotions shape how you develop a model and how you use the model to understand further observations. If you can understand this, you can compensate accordingly.

You have an emotion about every given topic or situation. That emotion permeates through your behaviour, and there's not much you can do to prevent yourself communicating how you feel. Over time people sense it, and it's usually not from what you say. It may be from the **way** you say things: the tone of your voice or the rhythm of your speech. It may also be from what you don't say, or it may be from your body language.

Consider what the great psychologist William James had to say more than a hundred years ago on how our bodies react to emotion and how far we can go in 'faking it':

… the changes are so indefinitely numerous and subtle that the entire organism may be called a sounding-board, which every change of consciousness, however slight, may reverberate. The various permutations and combinations of which these organic activities are susceptible make it abstractly impossible that no shade of emotion, however slight, should be without a bodily reverberation as unique, when taken in its totality, as in the mental mood itself. The immense number of parts modified in each emotion is what makes it so difficult for us to reproduce in cold blood the total and integral expression of any one of them. We may catch the trick with the voluntary muscles, but fail with the skin, glands, heart, and other viscera. Just as an artificially imitated sneeze lacks something of the reality, so the attempt to imitate an emotion in the absence of its normal instigating cause is apt to be rather 'hollow'. (James 1899)

Clearly William James didn't think you can get away with fooling people on a regular basis. At best trying to communicate something different from what you feel works in the short term. But it becomes an increasingly consuming activity over time. Eventually people pick up on it and doubt your sincerity.

The best thing you can do is understand how you feel about something and why you feel that way. While you'll probably have a tough time lying about how you feel, you might be able to rethink your attitude. You'll get much further by doing that.

MANAGING YOUR ATTITUDE

William James wrote a lot about emotion and attitude. On managing attitude he made the following observation: 'Human beings, by changing the inner attitudes of their minds, can change the outer aspects of their lives.' (James 1899)

High achievers know this and they use it to their advantage. They may not be able to change reality. And they may not be able to **hide** how they feel. But they can change their perspective and their focus. They can thereby **change** how they feel, and consequently how they react. Managing your attitude not only leads to higher levels of productivity, but what's more important, it leads to higher levels of wellbeing.

Randy Rose, who was Chief Operating Officer at Energizer Holdings before becoming CEO of Enzymatic Therapy, told me: 'Sure, I manage my attitude. For example, I do this when a huge challenge is dropped upon me. I cannot necessarily take something from a sorry state today and make it great, but I can make it a little better today, still better tomorrow, and so on. And I can certainly change my attitude, so that instead of seeing something as a catastrophe, I see it as something I can improve little by little. In other words, instead of seeing this huge insurmountable problem before me, I rethink my attitude to view it as a series of smaller problems that I can solve one at a time. I find that this overrides any panic sensation that might be my initial reaction.'

Randy went on to say: 'I encourage people in my organization to try to view things differently. Put things in a positive light – not by fooling yourself about the facts, but changing your perspective. For example, when something seems unpleasant in the short term, think about how it fits into a larger context. Another example is: when you are faced with a problem for which you have no immediate solution, remind yourself that just because you don't know the answer today, [it] doesn't mean you won't know it tomorrow. Remind yourself that in the past you have been able to solve similar problems even if the solution didn't come to you right away.'

David Novak is CEO of Yum! Brands. Because his family moved around constantly as he was growing up, he had to get good at making new friends and dealing with new situations.

He reasons that most of our fears are about things that never come to pass. The remainder of our fears are about things that turn out to be quite different from what we anticipate. You can't do away with your fears, but you can learn to keep them in check. (Novak and Boswell 2007)

'That kind of thinking will take you a long way to a happier out-look and hence a higher level of productivity. I was really pleased to see one of the teams in my company adopt the slogan "we refuse to be miserable". This is not to suggest the team has set out to go through the work day with blinders on. Rather, this team has cho-sen to view the facts in the context of a bigger picture.'[5]

You can change your perspective and you can also change your focus. How much importance do you want to attribute to a particu-lar event – or what aspect of the event do you want to bring to the forefront?

Managing your attitude is not a question of ignoring the facts; it's a question of managing your perception of events. And with the right attitude you can look to set up processes that work in your favour.

SETTING IN MOTION PROCESSES THAT RUN WITHOUT YOUR ATTENTION

Gary Stockman is president of Porter Novelli, a market communi-cations firm based in New York City and with offices in several countries. Gary told me an interesting story to illustrate how he learned the power of getting things running on their own so that he could then move on to something else.

'In the course of my life I've picked up lessons in time manage-ment in various situations. One of the places where I learned the most was in a restaurant kitchen where I worked towards the end of my high school years. One of the things I learned there by watching people that were really good was the importance of set-ting in motion things that could then run by themselves without your attention. This would then allow you to tend to other things.'

'I learned this the hard way. During my first week at work I would get order after order and would get absolutely snowed under. Then I observed the people who seemed able to make a kitchen run smoothly even though they received exactly the same number of

---

[5] Exclusive discussion with Randy Rose, March 2008.

orders as me. What I found was that the people who knew what they were doing would set in motion things that did not require a lot of their attention thereafter. This allowed them to do other things. For example, they would start one order frying and then turn their attention to things that required their active intervention.'

TIP #2

By setting up processes to run by themselves, you free yourself to do other things. Then if you have to fight fires, those processes that can run without you aren't affected by your inattention.

'I have since applied this principle everywhere I can. I've used it throughout my career, whether as a journalist or in communications and public relations. As CEO I now look for things that I can set in motion or that I can act as a catalyst in getting started, but that don't require my active intervention after that. Then I devote my time to things that require my attention. In my role as CEO, that would be a lot of meetings, and a lot of personal interactions with clients or staff.'

Gary thought for a moment. Then he summed it up. 'That restaurant experience was very formative for me.'[6]

Delegating is one way of setting in motion processes that then run without your attention. When you have other people working for you, the more you can hand off to them, the more you can pay attention to other matters. This being the case, the right thing to do is to put together a team of people you can count on to get things done. Put effort into nurturing a trusting relationship with the team. Once that's in place, delegating tasks is no problem at all.

Still another example that illustrates this concept is the familiar case of a boy coming to his mother for help with homework.

---

[6] Exclusive discussion with Gary Stockman, March 2008.

If the mother actually does the homework for her son, the result is much less powerful than if the mother puts the effort into teaching her son the good habits that allow him to work out problems on his own. Teaching the son to do homework on his own is setting in motion a process the mother will not have to tend to later.

Rather than fall in love with a process and try to 'own' it, set it up so that you become dispensable down the line. Setting processes in motion to then run on their own is a great idea. And you can do even better if you manage to set up processes that have positive outputs and that feed into one another.

PUTTING IN PLACE VIRTUOUS CYCLES

Most people know the term 'vicious cycle', which identifies a system in which one negative action feeds another negative action. That second action then feeds the first one, and so on. Each time around, the actions and their effects rise in intensity, resulting in a downward spiral.

For example, a boss suspects her employee of slacking off – not doing the job when the boss isn't looking. She confronts the underling in a way that causes him embarrassment. The underling then gets upset, and feels less motivated. Each time, the boss gets angrier, because the employee does less when alone. And, each time this happens, the employee feels increasingly humiliated, making him less motivated. So he works less and less, and the boss gets more and more angry.

Needless to say, nobody wants to be caught in a vicious cycle. They're painful when you're in one and they're hard to escape. But what about a system in which the actions are positive – a system that also mounts in intensity each time around, and in which the positive effects cause an upward spiral?

Does that exist? It surely does, and it's called a **virtuous cycle.**

Let's start with a simple case. The following familiar example illustrates a virtuous cycle. The more you pay attention to your kids, the more pleasant they become. The more pleasant they become, the more inclined you are to pay attention to them.

The same is true of people of all ages. The more you listen to somebody and really get into what it is they are trying to tell you, the better they become at communicating, and the better you understand each other. The better they communicate, the more you understand them, and the more you want to listen to them.

Just as you can create a virtuous cycle through good communication, you can also achieve an upward spiral of personal development. If you set small personal goals and accomplish them, you will feel more confident the next time you set out to do something. You then set more challenging goals, and reaching them gives you more confidence, and so on. In fact, you are learning to count on yourself first by achieving small goals and then building up to increasingly larger goals.

My favourite example of a virtuous cycle comes from David Smétanine. But first let's put this in context. As the result of a car accident in 1995, David was left a tetraplegic, which means he has no use of his legs and only partial use of his arms. After several months in hospital he decided to do something new with his life. So he set up virtuous cycles involving swimming, university studies, and planning a professional career. As soon as he could, he started training to swim at a competitive level. Working out several hours a day helped clear his mind for studies. The studies set him up for a professional career. The intellectual activity of working towards a business degree built up a need for a good workout in the pool. One thing fed into another and they all had positive results.

What became of David? In 2004 he won a bronze medal in the Athens Paralympics, and in 2008 he won two gold medals and two silver medals in the Paralympics in Peking. In the meantime he got an MBA and he has also become an elected official in France.

Not everybody thinks to create upward spirals. It's worth keeping this notion in mind and looking for as many situations as possible in which to put it to use. The same goes for sustainable processes.[7]

---

[7] Exclusive discussion with David Smétanine, April 2010.

STRIVING FOR SUSTAINABILITY

Boxers who come out swinging might win the first round, but unless they land a knockout blow early on, they're bound to lose. They will tire much more quickly than their opponents. A marathon runner who starts out sprinting might break out ahead of the pack in the beginning, but will quickly drop off from exhaustion. Likewise, a business that starts out with a large investment and pours all its money into landing the first few sales will probably wind up bankrupt. To prevent this it must also put in place both the capacity to deliver on those sales and the organisation to go out and get still more sales.

Starting something that can't possibly continue might bring you early victory and the accompanying thrill. But eventually it will fall on its face and require your full attention – quite possibly at a time when you can least afford to divert your focus. If you're lucky you can avoid complete disaster, but in most such cases you wind up with failure – and worse off than when you started. A process that is not sustainable is an emergency waiting to happen.

TIP #3

Setting up sustainable systems will minimize the number of problems you'll have to deal with down the line.

As obvious as this seems, people frequently fool themselves into thinking that somehow things will work themselves out in the long run. They wind up working so frantically in the short term that exhaustion is a certain outcome. They seem to ignore the inevitable. Ray Titus, CEO of United Franchising Group, told me: 'Sometimes you have to abstain from taking a short-term gain in order to put together a process that works better in the long run. Don't think in terms of quick fixes. Think in terms of lasting processes.'[8]

---

[8] Exclusive discussion with Ray Titus, July 2008.

This principle applies to just about anything you do.

You need to have sustainable systems health-wise. For example, if you simply go on a crash diet, the chances are that you will gain all your weight back afterwards by going back to your old eating habits. If, on the other hand, you change your eating habits, you can sustain weight loss.

You also need sustainability in your intellectual pursuits. You can't just study biology in an all-night cram session and expect to retain the knowledge in the long term.

And you need sustainability in your work–life balance. If your way of living doesn't allow you to nurture your family, the chances are that you'll pay for it in the long run. Workaholics eventually hit a brick wall, because they've put all their effort into work and ignored everything else around them.

Finally, to see how well sustainability works in business, consider Southwest Airlines, where the leaders made sure that profit always accompanied growth. CEO Herb Kelleher chose not to gain market share by moving into markets where Southwest would be less profitable. He knew that, even though short-term growth might look good to investors, any strategy that brought about growth but diluted profits at the same time was not sustainable. (Freiberg and Freiberg 1997)

If your habits are sustainable you take a long-term view and can think of problem solving as a skill that can be improved over time. Don't just solve one problem; try to solve groups of problems.

SOLVING A CLASS OF PROBLEMS INSTEAD OF JUST THE PROBLEM AT HAND

When faced with a challenge, instead of viewing it in isolation, you can view it in the context of a class of problems. For example, let's say you are preparing a speech on the best strategy for your company to adopt over the next year. To accomplish this, you first need to evaluate different strategies and decide which one is best. Then you have to develop the presentation. And finally you must deliver the talk. You aren't sure how long it will take you to find the right strategy. You aren't sure how long it will take to develop the presentation. And you aren't sure how much time you need to deliver it.

You can view the problem as unique, or you can view it as a member of one or more categories of problems. Using the category approach, you would compare the task with other situations where you had to find a new strategy. Or, if you personally have never worked on a task in this category, look to other people who have. Do this for each of the problem components. In the case just described the three components are: finding the strategy, developing a presentation on the strategy, and delivering the presentation.

K. Surivakumar (Suri) is CEO of American Reprographics. He took the company from $25 million in revenue to almost $1 billion in just 10 years.

Suri groups problems into categories. If you think of the problem at hand as practice for other similar problems that are likely to come your way in the future, you can kill two birds with one stone.[9]

There are at least three advantages to taking the category view. First, it puts the immediate problem into a different perspective, and allows you to see beyond the obstacle in front of you. Right away this provides some emotional relief. Second, by taking the category view you can view the problem as practice for solving similar problems in the future. In other words, overcoming the present obstacle positions you to better overcome similar obstacles later on. A third advantage to viewing a problem in the context of one or more categories results from comparing it to similar problems. You can make more accurate predictions about the amount of time and the resources you will need to overcome the problem at hand.

Daniel Kahneman, leading psychology researcher, has spent a lot of time working to demonstrate this last point. He calls the two broad ways of viewing a problem the 'inside view', which means

---

[9] Exclusive discussion with K. Surivakumar, March 2008.

that you look only at the problem in front of you, and the 'outside view', which means that you view the problem within a category. Kahneman says that by taking the outside view you can eliminate some of the biases that are inevitable when you consider just the problem at hand. The outside view allows you to compare it with similar problems and to take a more objective view when deciding how best to approach it and estimating how much time and effort are required to solve it (Kahneman and Tversky 2000).

Kahneman was so good at showing how biased we are that he won the Nobel prize in economics. It turns out that we don't make decisions rationally and that, to some extent, we can overcome bias by applying methods such as viewing problems by category.

Some of what Kahneman discovered through research, many CEOs do naturally. K. Surivakumar (Suri), CEO of American Reprographics, told me that when looking ahead to see what challenges might lie in front of him, instead of trying to be all knowing he prepares himself for what **might** lie ahead by thinking about categories of problems that he **might** encounter. He views any immediate challenge as practice for solving future problems. This is not to say that he doesn't consider immediate problems serious in and of themselves. 'I take the task in front of me very seriously,' Suri told me. 'But I also take it apart to see the components that can help me in the future. For example, if solving the immediate problem involves overcoming some fear I have, I view that as practice.'[10]

The most effective people are good problem solvers because they take a methodical approach. They are conscious of their approach, and they know it can be used over and over in different situations. Effective people categorise problems, and they work on root causes rather than symptoms.

SOLVING PROBLEMS AT THEIR SOURCE

In order to find the source of a problem we first have to see clearly. For enlightenment we can turn again to Daniel Kahneman and other cognitive psychologists. They have demonstrated some of the

---

[10] Exclusive discussion with K. Surivakumar, March 2008.

ways in which we are biased both in problem identification and in selecting a solution. One source of bias is the **illusion of optimism**. We tend to be excessively optimistic in our planning or in our analysis of our position with respect to competitors. A more common term for this phenomenon is **wishful thinking.**

Anchoring is another source of bias. Here we start out with an assumption. From then on, all thinking revolves around that anchor point. This commonly occurs in business planning. Executives select an objective and then write a plan. All assumptions that go into the plan – and all actions to be taken – magically support exactly that objective. In this situation, planners tend to ignore anything that proves the objective unreasonable.

This kind of bias was demonstrated in its purest form by an experiment conducted by Wilson et al. (1996) in which participants were asked to write down the last four digits of their social security numbers. Then they were each asked to state whether they thought the number of physicians and surgeons listed in a local telephone directory was higher or lower than that number. Finally they were asked to estimate the actual number of physicians and surgeons listed. The estimates strongly correlated with the last four digits of the participants' social security numbers. Go figure.

TIP #4

To solve a problem at its source you have to minimise the bias in your thinking. Good problem solvers are methodical, and they recognise their approach as repeatable.

Yet another common bias in problem identification is our tendency towards supporting a one-sided argument. Brenner, Koehler, and Tversky (1996) demonstrated this nicely in the following study. Experimenters gave four groups of participants different pieces of information from a real jury trial and then asked them to guess what the jury had decided. One group heard both the defendant's and the plaintiff's arguments. Each of two of the other groups heard the arguments presented by only one of the sides. The fourth group got both sides of the story plus some background information.

The two groups with equal information from both sides were most accurate in estimating what the jury decided. That makes sense. But then there were findings that appeared less rational. The two groups with just one side's argument each guessed that the jury had decided in favour of the arguments that their own group had heard. Even though the groups hearing only one side of the story knew that they were biased, they were unable to compensate for it. Worse still, when experimenters asked the participants how confident they were in their estimation of the jury's decision, the answers were surprising. Those who had heard only one side were much more confident in their analysis than were those who had heard both sides. That is, the groups who knew they were skewed were still more confident in their selection. This scary finding shows how flawed our thinking can be when we assess a situation.

To minimise bias, it's good to have a methodology. In the 1950s, a couple of decades before Kahneman and Tversky's work was published, Charles Kepner and Benjamin Tregoe were commissioned by the United States military to investigate problem solving. They found that many people were really bad at identifying root causes. These people ignored important facts and were generally biased from the outset. Bad problem solvers were not methodical.

Kepner and Tregoe also found that some people were very good at spotting the root cause and selecting solutions. These people thought through the challenge in front of them and were able to identify their problem solving process. They were conscious of their approach, which they recognised as repeatable, and which they applied to all challenges. Starting from what they learned from these people, Kepner and Tregoe (1981) put together a method for problem solving.

Andrew Graham is now CEO of the consulting firm founded by Kepner and Tregoe, which specialises in mentoring companies on rational analysis. Of all the CEOs I interviewed, Andrew could best describe the importance of solving problems at their source. He told me that a useful way of defining a problem is as 'a situation in which something has gone wrong without explanation'.

Andrew went on to say: 'Problem analysis is carried out using what we call "cause and effect" thinking. This is the inductive reasoning process we carry out naturally. Given a few unexplained observations, people just need to have an explanation – even an inaccurate one. Because we're only human, we need a methodical approach to compensate for bias. You need to extract the essential information from a troublesome situation, setting aside everything that's confusing or irrelevant.'

'The source of a problem becomes apparent when you understand the problem in four dimensions: identity, location, timing, and magnitude,' Andrew said. 'In other words, you need to identify what you're trying to explain, where it's observed, when it occurs, and how serious it is.'[11]

Of course the best case is when you're able to head off a problem before it gets out of hand. One way to head off problems early is to go out and ask other people for their opinions. Find out how they view the situation and what they think might lie down the road. Do they have ideas about how to solve the problems you're facing? When you take the category view you can take advantage of advice from other people who have overcome similar obstacles. While it certainly is good to learn from your own mistakes, it's far better to learn from somebody else's.

SEEKING ADVICE

When Sandra Kurtzig started her company ASK, she put in place a virtual board of directors. The company was very small, so it was not a formal board. It was a group of people who could give her fresh ideas and guide her. (Kurtzig with Parker 1994) Gert Boyle did the same thing when she began running Columbia Sportswear. She set up a group of people who had opinions that were different from her own, but that she respected.[12] In both of these cases, the people on the virtual board of directors were not paid in the early days. Because these two women went out and solicited advice, they got it. And they got it at no cost.

---

[11] Exclusive discussion with Andrew Graham, September 2008.
[12] Exclusive discussion with Getrude Boyle, August 2008.

Or take for example Frank Stewart. He got out of the Navy as an officer in 1959 and immediately took over the family funeral services business. As we learned in the first few paragraphs of Chapter 1, Frank built the company from a 15-person operation to a publicly traded multinational with 6000 employees. Today Stewart Enterprises is the second-largest death care provider in the world. How did he do it?

According to Frank, the best thing he did was to get advice from several people he called his mentors. In particular, he told me, 'I had the benefit of an industrial psychologist for 27 years. He was probably the most influential part of my life, because he taught me how to put round pegs in round holes and square ones in square holes. He said that everybody, without exception, is different. There are no two alike.'

'The key to success is building a team by putting the right people in the right jobs,' he said. 'This may sound obvious, but that industrial psychologist really brought the point home and caused me to internalise that fundamental point, which made all the difference in the world. The business benefited, and people found much more satisfaction doing what they were uniquely suited to do. And it's all because I went out and asked people for their opinions, a lot of which were given to me free.'[13]

Effective people also look for help from others who have been in their position, or a similar position, before them. Charlice Byrd says: 'Seeking advice from people that have already been through the fire will make you a better person. There's nothing wrong with having a mentor, somebody who's already been through some of the difficult situations you're facing. Their wisdom and knowledge is incredible.'

A House Representative in Georgia, for the third consecutive year Charlice was named one of the 25 most influential Asians in that state by the Asian Times Magazine. Influential she is, but she also knows she has to allow herself to be influenced. 'People who go off on their own and don't solicit advice, or who don't align themselves with other people, rarely succeed,' Charlice says.

---

[13] Exclusive discussion with Frank Stewart, April 2008.

'I think in most cases these people are very egotistical, and they pay a heavy price for being that way.'[14]

The lesson I learned from the CEOs I interviewed is to seek advice from anybody who can give you good ideas. Don't be too shy or too proud to go out and ask other people what they think. And, as we shall now see, it is especially important to solicit ideas from those who have a vested interest. They are personally concerned about your success, and consequently have probably come up with ideas of their own. What's more, on an emotional level it comforts them to feel involved.

CONSIDERING ALL STAKEHOLDERS

Part of time management is allocating time to spend with the people who have a vested interest in what you're doing. Steve Simpson was CEO of Extended Systems, which was one of the first market leaders in mobile software products. He told me: 'You have to figure out how you're going to interact with various stakeholders and how much time you're going to invest with each group of them. When you're running a company, this means spending time with at least the following groups: customers, employees, investors, and the community. The general lesson to your readers is: don't ignore anybody who has a vested interest in what you're doing. Let the different players know what you're thinking and seek out their opinions.'[15]

As part of his planning process, Randy Rose of Schwabe North America writes future annual reports. The process of thinking ahead and putting his ideas into the form of an annual report creates a vision for the company. Not only does this exercise help him plan, it also helps him get good ideas from everybody who has a stake in the business. What's more, it keeps stakeholders informed about company direction. Randy told me: 'When I write my future annual reports, I solicit input from the different stakeholders. This serves two purposes: it gives me ideas I might not have obtained otherwise, and it gives the other players a sense of involvement and ownership.'[16]

[14] Exclusive discussion with Charlice Byrd, May 2008.
[15] Exclusive discussion with Steve Simpson, March 2008.
[16] Exclusive discussion with Randy Rose, March 2008.

As CEO of Hibernia Corporation, Steve Hansel was on the line for $17 billion in assets.

Steve cautions not to go off the deep end with your own ideas. Make sure others are on board.[17]

But on an individual level the stakeholders are not just the people or entities you're involved with in business. The people who have a vested interest in your personal life are also stakeholders. Listen to what Janice Chaffin, president of the consumer business in Symantec, has to say about the importance of considering those closest to you. She told me: 'I think most people struggle with maintaining the right balance between family and work. Where you draw that line is a personal choice. But in all cases you need to be clear to all stakeholders where you draw the line; and then you need to really respect the boundaries you put in place.'

Janice continued: 'I've seen people take on a demanding job and spend almost all of their time working. A few years later their family breaks up. I have also seen people who take on a tough job and make a conscious decision with the consent of their family to work like crazy for two years and then ease up or change jobs. This works, if all stakeholders are informed ahead of time.'[18]

SLOWING DOWN TO GO FASTER

When faced with challenges, we tend to forget the value of stepping back to look at the big picture. In some cases the urgent matter might be something not worth doing in the first place. In fact, the urgent task frequently squeezes out something more important – our top priorities.

There's an opportunity cost to everything we do. By working on one thing, we shut out the opportunity to work on something else. In a case where we let an urgent task divert our attention away from something more important, we pay a high opportunity cost for tending to the emergency. And it's not by choice. It's because

---

[17] Exclusive discussion with Steve Hansel, March 2008.
[18] Exclusive discussion with Janice Chaffin, March 2008.

it was forced upon us. In other cases when we're in a hurry to do something it may be the right thing to do, but we don't take the time to think through the best way of doing it. Rushing into the task is suboptimal. In both situations – when you do the wrong thing because it's thrust upon you, or when you do the right thing the wrong way – the best way to speed up is to first slow down.

This is not something that comes naturally to most people. In a lot of cases you need to show progress in the short term. Sometimes people dive into something because they think the quicker they start, the quicker they finish.

Randy Rose said: 'If you don't slow down to assess where it is you're going, you'll never be able to speed up. If you simply go through the business day working on the tasks at hand without taking the time to assess what's really important, you may not be doing the right things. For example, when you go to work in the morning, instead of immediately going to your inbox to react to mail, take ten minutes to think about what you really want to accomplish during the day.'

Randy went on: 'and when you know where you're going, and you know the task at hand is going to get you there, you really need to think about how best to accomplish that task. It took me a long time to fully embrace the idea of slowing down to go faster.'[19]

Lucas Skoczkowski of Redknee put it this way: 'It takes most people a long time to really internalize the concept that often to go faster you have to slow down. You have to do a lot of things that aren't intuitive. Several years ago I thought that by doing things faster and doing more things, I would create more value. But, over time, I have come to realize that you get a lot more value when you slow down to figure out where you are going and plot out the best way to get there.'[20]

We just went over 11 powerful notions. These are good ideas that have the potential to make a big difference. But, until you make them your own, they don't have much value. Now is a good time to slow down and make these concepts work for you.

---

[19] Exclusive discussion with Randy Rose, March 2008.
[20] Exclusive discussion with Lucas Skoczkowski, April 2008.

3 MAKING IT WORK FOR YOU

Too many people share the following frustration. They go to time management training or read books on personal effectiveness. Then a month or so later they see no difference. The problem is that they don't internalise the ideas and turn them into habit. Nobody can wave a magic wand over your head and make you change. You have to do the work yourself.

What I can do is to help you turn those ideas into automatic behaviour. I'm going to do this by suggesting a set of good time management habits. I'll also provide a method you can use to make the changes yourself. Master The Moment consists of six steps. For each step, there are two habits, a whole lot of ideas, and at least one technique. I like to use the acronym HIT, which stands for **habits**, **ideas**, and **techniques**.

INTERNALISING IDEAS

Before changing behaviour, you first have to accept the underlying ideas and make them your own. Psychologists tell us that when confronted with a new idea we react in one of the following ways:

- **Rejecting it:** We turn it away outright.

- **Introjecting it:** We take it on, but not wholeheartedly.

- **Integrating it:** We accept it as if it were our own.

Even though many of the ideas in this book will be familiar to you, it's worthwhile revisiting them in this new context. Please take the time to fully consider all the concepts we discuss and to work them into your own thinking. Work them into your own value system. Integrate them. Once you've done this, you can start turning them into automatic behaviour.

Maintaining autonomy

Later in this book we'll talk about delegating. We'll cover ways of increasing the chances that somebody else will internalise your ideas and take ownership of something you ask them to do. One of the leading schools of thought on human motivation, Self Determination Theory (SDT), explains how best to delegate (Deci with Flaste 1995). Provide a rationale, acknowledge that the task might be difficult or uninteresting, and minimise the pressure so that the other person feels a greater sense of choice. If you do this, you stand a greater chance that this person will accept the task and even take it on as his or her own. The more other people remain autonomous in accepting new tasks, the better they will perform. In fact, SDT founders Edward Deci and Richard Ryan make a distinction between internalisation and integration. Internalisation refers to the process of taking in a value or regulation. Integration is the process of working the value or regulation into one's inner self, so that subsequently it will emanate from one's deepest regions.

TIP #5

The freer you feel in your choice to take on a new idea, the more thoroughly you'll integrate that idea.

While this concept applies to delegating to others, the same principles also apply to the situation where you're internalising ideas that you learn on your own. The freer you feel in choosing to take on the ideas, the more thoroughly you'll integrate them. Threats to this freedom don't just come from the outside. They may also be caused by internal forces. For example, if your ego is attached to a belief, you'll accept it out of pride, and not necessarily because you really like it. Similarly if you take on an idea out of a sense of guilt or obligation, you in fact coerce yourself into accepting it.

Internalising through teaching

One way of internalising an idea is to teach it to somebody else. James Ravannack learned this the hard way. 'When I was 24 years old I had problems with drug addiction and alcoholism,' he told me. 'I spent 47 days in a rehab hospital, soul searching and trying to set some direction in my life. That was a very successful year for me business-wise, but it was a horrible year for me personally.'

'I realised I was killing myself, so I quit drinking and taking drugs,' James said. 'I decided to start helping other people. I did so by coaching wrestling and helping kids. From then on, I made sure I was doing the right things every step of the way. I didn't worry about what other people were doing; I just worried about what I did.'

When James Ravannack co-founded his first company, there were five employees. When he left, there were 4000 and the company's market capitalisation was over $3 billion. The company had become Superior Energy Services, a Fortune 1000 company. James now runs Compliance Technology Group and is involved in several other businesses. He is also president of the US Olympic Wrestling Committee.

As a young adult James overcame drug addiction. Through that experience he learned that one good way of internalising a new idea is to teach it to somebody else.

He continued: 'I met a man during that process who told me, "I don't care what you do, the one thing you'll have forever is your name. Whatever you do with it, it's the one thing people will remember you for: your name. Build a reputation on doing the right things. All you really have is your name." That advice stuck with me.'

'I helped myself by helping other people,' James summarised. 'I find it's the same thing with learning: one good way of learning something is to teach it. If you teach something, you automatically learn it – and you take it for granted, because you don't realise that's what you're doing. So I became a wrestling coach, and I started counseling kids to let them know what my story was.'[1]

One way of internalising the ideas presented in this book is to share them with other people. Reinforce what you've learned by teaching it. You'll benefit and so will the other people.

ACQUIRING NEW HABITS

Throughout this book we discuss ways in which we are biased in our thinking. You need to recognise your skews and find ways of compensating – to make a conscious effort to override a subconscious system.

The same goes for bad habits. Overcoming bad routines and replacing them with good automatic behaviour requires work. The good news is that this is a process you can get better at through practice.

The nature of habit

A habit is a behavioural response acquired through repetition. The behaviour becomes automatic. Given the proper trigger, it is then performed with little or no conscious effort. We need habits, because we simply can't think of everything at once. When we walk we aren't conscious of the multitude of small acts we carry out to perform the walking procedure. Normal functioning requires that we learn to perform such procedures automatically, with very little conscious effort. When a procedure becomes a habit we are free to put our cognitive effort to other uses.

Neurologists have discovered that memories for habits and skills are different from memories of facts, and use different parts of the brain. One nice feature of habit is that once you have formed a habit you don't have to consciously remember the whole procedure. This dramatically cuts down on the mental processing you have to carry out. On the other hand, learning a new behavioural procedure requires extensive repetition. Learning not to perform such patterns once they've become habit is often even more difficult.

---

[1] Exclusive discussion with James Ravannack, April 2009.

But regaining an old habit can occur quickly – sometimes one or a very small number of cues can reactivate old habits.

Nobody really knows for sure what the neurological basis for habit is. A good deal of evidence points to the basal ganglia as playing an essential role in procedural or habit learning. It can be shown that this part of the brain changes during acquisition of a new routine. Furthermore, lesions in the basal ganglia make it difficult or even impossible for patients to perform procedural tasks (Graybiel 2005). Researchers have these kinds of general ideas. But they are still trying to figure out exactly what neural processes allow us to develop habits or to break them once they are formed.

It would be nice if scientists came up with a pill that made it easier to modify our behaviour. But unfortunately there's nothing like that on the horizon. We really haven't improved on the old-fashioned techniques for acquiring or breaking habits.

Developing new habits

A hundred years ago American psychologist and philosopher Williams James wrote a good deal on the subject of habit. He said that habits build up over time and become automatic, so that you no longer have to think about them to set them in motion. Changing automatic behaviour involves pitting two hostile powers against one another. The old procedure has the advantage of being more deeply rooted. To replace it with a new habit, you have to combat the old inclinations long enough for the new behaviour to develop even stronger roots.

According to James (1899), the best way to break old habits and take on new ones is to follow these three basic rules:

- **Launch yourself with as strong and decided an initiative as possible.** Put yourself in situations that encourage the new behaviour and create circumstances that are incompatible with the old behaviour. Where appropriate, you might take a public pledge to change. Doing these things will give you some momentum in the beginning, and push away the temptation to fall back to your old ways. For every day you postpone a breakdown, the less likely it becomes that it will ever happen at all.

- **Never suffer an exception to occur until the new habit is securely rooted in your life.** Try not to let the new habits lose a battle against the old ones. Every time you give in slightly to the old procedures you undo a good deal of the effort you put into building the new ones. You need to have a series of uninterrupted successes with the new habits for them to become strong enough to override the nagging old habits.

- **Seize the very first possible opportunity to act on every resolution you make, and on every emotional prompting you may experience in the direction of the habits you aspire to gain.** You need to make the new habits automatic and forge their automatism into the brain. The more you exercise new behaviour, the quicker you develop the motor effect.

William James also said that it's important to keep the faculty of effort alive through a little gratuitous exercise every day. Do something every day for no other reason than that it's difficult. Doing so will raise your capacity for self control.

These ideas are consistent with the work of modern researcher Roy F. Baumeister, whose studies suggest that self-regulation is something like sports training. You tire of it and your capacity is diminished when you've done too much. But you can also build stamina through practice.

According to Baumeister et al. (2007), self-regulation often consumes a limited resource, rather like energy or strength. It creates a temporary state of ego depletion. Once you've reached that point, further efforts at self-regulation are less successful. The theory is that the ego depletion occurs because self-regulation overrides the ego's initial response, which is to act according to habit. Overcoming habit involves an internal battle between the first impulse and the new behaviour.

Experiments show that the effects of ego depletion do not impair one's abilities to perform a difficult task that does **not** require self control. For example, working on habits does not diminish your ability to solve straightforward mathematical problems or to memorise words. However, excessive self-regulation in one area does diminish one's capacity for self-regulation in a completely different area. So, for example, if you spend all day trying to correct your posture, your efforts to restrain drinking will be impaired in the evening. The important point for our discussion is that working on one habit diminishes your capacity to work on another in the same day.

TIP #6

Changing habits is something you can get better at through practice: if you practice self-regulation in one area, you become better at self-regulation in another area.

The good news, according to Baumeister, is that you can get better at developing new habits through practice. Self-regulation seems to be driven by a core capacity. If you perform exercises in one sphere, you become better at self-regulation in other spheres. For example, people who get good at dieting become well practised in self-regulation. These people will therefore have an increased capacity to develop good habits in time management.

Overriding habit

Now let's go back further in time, before William James. Over 200 years ago Benjamin Franklin developed an approach to changing habits. As a young adult seeking to straighten out his act, he compiled a list of 13 virtues, and gave a brief definition of each. These were character traits he took to be important, but in which he found himself lacking. He thought that nurturing these habits would bring about big improvements in his life. The list, taken from his autobiography, is shown in Table 3.1.

It's interesting to see what items Benjamin Franklin came up with, and to note how highly personal his list is. If you were to go through the same exercise, your list would probably look quite different. That's why, for the sake of this discussion, we aren't very concerned with what Franklin thought were good character traits. More important is his approach to developing such a list and to changing habits accordingly.

Table 3.1 Benjamin Franklin's list of 13 virtues (Franklin 1993)

1.	*Temperance*	Eat not to dulness. Drink not to elevation.
2.	*Silence*	Speak not but what may benefit others or yourself. Avoid trifling conversation.
3.	*Order*	Let all your things have their places. Let each part of your business have its time.
4.	*Resolution*	Resolve to perform what you ought. Perform without fail what you resolve.
5.	*Frugality*	Make no expense but to do good to others or yourself: i.e. waste nothing.
6.	*Industry*	Lose no time. Be always employed in something useful. Cut off all unnecessary actions.
7.	*Sincerity*	Use no hurtful deceit. Think innocently and justly; and if you speak, speak accordingly.
8.	*Justice*	Wrong none by doing injuries or omitting the benefits that are your duty.
9.	*Moderation*	Avoid extremes. Forebear resenting injuries so much as you think they deserve.
10.	*Cleanliness*	Tolerate no uncleanness in body, clothes, or habitation.
11.	*Tranquility*	Be not disturbed at trifles, or at accidents common or unavoidable.
12.	*Chastity*	Rarely use venery but for health or offspring; never to dulness, weakness, or the injury of your own or another's peace or reputation.
13.	*Humility*	Imitate Jesus and Socrates.

The first thing to note about Franklin's approach is that he consulted people around him on what virtues should make his list. For example, he didn't include humility until a friend pointed out to him that this was an area where he could use improvement. Adding it brought the number of virtues to 13, which, as you will see, turned out to be a convenient number.

Franklin ordered his list in such a way that improvement on virtues higher up facilitated improvement on those lower down. For example, if he improved on temperance, silence would come more easily.

He carried his list with him, and every day he would note how many times he violated each of the virtues. At first he was surprised to see how 'faulty' his behaviour was, but he resolved to make improvements. The daily rating allowed him to measure progress.

He decided to focus effort on one virtue at a time, and to try to develop the right habits in that area so that the desired behaviour became automatic. To this end, each week Franklin would concentrate on improving one of the virtues. He would work through the entire list in a 13-week cycle, and he could complete four such cycles per year. He went through one year in that way, and then progressively slackened off.

Of course he never achieved the perfection he first set out for. For example, everybody knows that chastity never became one of his personality traits. But even though Franklin fell short of perfection – as would anybody else – his approach for developing good habits is worth considering. In fact, he noted in his autobiography that by working through this process he had discovered that, while perfection was unattainable, he could make big improvements.

This method comes from a young man who had run away from home, and who wanted to do something with his life. Following his work on habits, Benjamin Franklin went on to be a journalist, a business owner, a diplomat, a philosopher, and a founding father of the United States. His approach is certainly worth considering. As you will see, I've made it a cornerstone of Master The Moment.

Visualising

CEO of LifeLock, Todd Davis is a man whose picture is often seen in advertisements where he gives out his social security number.

Todd says he has managed to overcome bad habits by visualising. He creates a mental image of what he wants to be – or of where he wants to go. Then, to prevent himself from 'falling off the wagon', he frequently evokes that image as a reminder.

Another way of changing habits is through visualisation. There are two important aspects to this technique. One is drawing up a mental image of who you want to be. By doing this you develop a level of comfort with that image of yourself and the situation you want to be in. The second part is to set up mental reminders of what you're trying to accomplish. These reminders might be the mental images you've drawn up. Or they might be external cues, such as a list of goals you consult.

Todd Davis, CEO of LifeLock, talked to me about how he changed one of his nagging habits. He used to take on too much because he had a hard time saying 'no' to requests. 'In my transition from being somebody who would always say "yes" and take on whatever came my way, "visualizing" played an important role,' Todd told me. 'It becomes a self-fulfilling prophecy. If you tell yourself that you're going to have the discipline to reject things that are outside of your mission, you then see the payback, which in turn increases your ability to say "no" in the future. This makes up a virtuous cycle that reinforces your new discipline.'

Todd advises: 'Take the time to visualize your mission, or whatever you have to do. The more you do this the better you get at the process of visualizing. When you drive, you look down the road, rather than directly in front of you. This is analogous with how you go through life. You should look down the road.'

Todd summarised: 'All this might conflict with the style you have become accustomed to. But the new style will make you dramatically more effective.'[2]

---

[2] Exclusive discussion with Todd Davis, March 2008.

Visualisation has also worked for Paul Orfalea. A dyslexic, he had the hardest time learning to read. His problems were so pronounced that they prompted his Catholic schoolteachers to administer corporal punishment. He writes in his autobiography: 'Picturing myself owning my own business one day helped me navigate through my difficulties in the second grade. Even as Sister Sheila paddled me, I told myself that someday I would own my own business and have secretaries who would read for me.' Visualising helped Orfalea through tough times and he went on to be a very successful businessman. Among other things, he was founder of Kinko's® (now FedEx Office).

To stay focused on his goals, Paul Orfalea would list them in a notebook. He could then visualise his desired results by looking at what he wrote. Every six weeks or so, he would review his list and revise if necessary. Setting and maintaining goals is more like impressionist painting, he says. You can't be too precise because there's too much you don't know in the beginning. It makes more sense to allow yourself to adapt to what you learn. Don't fix an outcome, such as opening three new stores in the next three months. Instead, word the goal to be something like 'expand the business'. He advises: 'Keep your goals as anchor and then wander around among them, giving yourself plenty of room for error and experimentation.' (Orfalea and Marsh 2007)

TIP #7

Changing habits involves a constant struggle between firstimpulses and the desired behaviour. If you set up visible reminders of what you want to achieve, you reinforce the new behaviour in times when the struggle drags you down.

Former CEO of Entergy, Dan Packer, told me: 'When you're talking about becoming more effective, to a large extent we're talking about modifying behaviour. If you are somebody who comes in the morning and just decides what to do on the spot, and you want to become more organized and have a more studied approach, you have to modify your behavior. You have to acquire new habits.

To do so, you need as much reinforcement as possible. In order for the new habit to stick, you need to continuously see signs that the new path you're on leads to success and the old path leads to failure. Look for ways of reminding yourself through visible signs.'[3]

AN OVERVIEW OF THE SIX STEPS

We can lump the different elements of good time management into six big categories. Since good time management is a lifelong endeavour, we will call these 'steps' to lend them a sense of motion. This is not a science, and you'll never achieve perfection. However, if you continually follow this process, you will certainly see improvement in your personal effectiveness.

In the six chapters that follow we cover the six steps that you can take to improve your own time management (see Figure 3.1).

- **Identify yourself.** If you know what you want, and are comfortable with wanting it, focusing effort towards getting it will come naturally. And don't forget about people – you rely on them. How you fit in with people makes all the difference in how effective you are.

- **Energise.** Most people know that regular exercise, good eating habits, and a good night's sleep will give you more energy. But do they put that knowledge to work? Find out how high achievers make sure they have enough gas in the tank. Discover your biorhythms and make them work in your favour.

- **Prioritise.** Set goals, assign them priorities, and plan your work accordingly. Eliminate distractions, turning down things you don't have time for.

- **Optimise.** Find out where you're wasting time. Eliminate what you can, and try to fill the remaining dead time with useful activity. Block off time for focused effort. Get better at doing the things you do regularly: use tools, delegate, and get more out of meetings.

---

[3] Exclusive discussion with Dan Packer, October 2008.

- **Head off problems early.** Build solid processes that last. This frees you to think about the future. Look down the road for problems that might come your way. Head them off early.

- **Finish things.** Break your work into small chunks. Finish what you start, and hand it off to somebody in a way that allows the other person to see its value. In some cases it becomes clear that what you've started isn't worth finishing. In such situations, cut your losses.

Figure 3.1 The six steps to improving time management

At the end of each of the next six chapters I suggest two constructive habits to work on. To make this behaviour automatic, we will use an approach based on what we've learned from Benjamin Franklin, William James, and Roy Baumeister. We'll work on two habits at a time and set up visual reminders. To get started, try spending one week on each step, filling out the rating form every day at the end of that step's chapter. Once you get used to this process, you can get more rigorous, working on one habit at a time and using the techniques I discuss in the last chapter.

Are you ready to take the first step?

PART II:
SIX STEPS TO GOOD TIME
MANAGEMENT

4 IDENTIFY YOURSELF

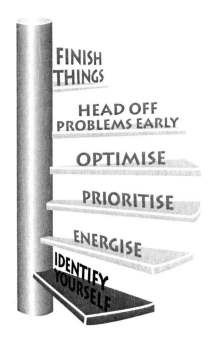

FINISH
THINGS

HEAD OFF
PROBLEMS EARLY

OPTIMISE

PRIORITISE

ENERGISE

IDENTIFY
YOURSELF

If you know what you want and are comfortable with your intention, you stand a much better chance of getting it. People who know what they're after aim in the right direction. If they're completely at ease with their goals, they also apply a great deal of positive energy towards the target. Quite simply, the more you work towards what you really want, the more effectively you work.

And let's not forget that, to be effective, you need to recognise the importance of other people. What kinds of people should you surround yourself with? Where do you fit with respect to others?

SETTING YOUR COURSE

I spoke to Patrick Quinlan, CEO of Ochsner Health Systems, which with 10,000 people is the largest private employer in Louisiana. Pat told me: 'I believe it was Socrates who said "the uninspected life is not worth living". I take that to heart, and try to live an "inspected life". This means defining a mission, and keeping an eye on why you do things and how those things relate to your overall mission. In the broader sense, time management is not really about managing hours. It's more about how you manage the end to which you are using those hours.'

He went on: 'Your energy and your personal effectiveness flow from your sense of purpose. Understanding and developing that sense of purpose is not intuitive. It's usually a product of introspection, and being aware of your situation, and integrating all those things.'

Pat was jogging on the treadmill in his office as we spoke. Exercise gives him more energy and increases his attention. He also does some of his best thinking while working out. 'It takes a long time and a lot of introspection to figure out where you want to go,' he continued. 'But the sooner you start your soul-searching, the sooner you'll figure out where you want to be, and the sooner you'll get on the right track to getting there.'

'Most people sleep around seven hours a night,' Pat estimated. 'That leaves them with around 120 waking hours a week. But it's not just the number of hours that counts – your attitude towards those hours is hugely important. People who are engrossed in what they do because they find it so rewarding will think there just aren't enough hours in the day. What's more, they will work a great number of those hours very productively. Conversely, somebody who resents doing what they're doing will put in fewer hours, and those hours will be relatively unproductive. They work in the spirit of compromise. They don't enjoy what they do – they do it only because they have to.'

I could tell he had given a lot of thought to the subject of time management – and that he was excited about the topic. Pat went on to say: 'Great artists, for example, don't say "Oh my God! Do I have to go to the studio again?" In fact, you can't get them **out** of the studio, because they love what they're doing. Michelangelo wasn't looking for a vacation. He was driven by passion.'

TIP #8

Be selective in where you put your efforts. Choose to spend most of your time doing those things you're most passionate about.

'Have you found something worthy of spending your life on? If you haven't, then that's your most pressing problem.' Pat advises: 'The first thing is to ask if you are doing something you really want to do. If not, do what you can to change that. The first step on your way to good time management is finding something worth spending your time on. By making the right choices early, some of the other problems become moot, because you are driven and have a sense of energy. The positive energy you bring to what you do makes you more effective, and consequently brings you more satisfaction. In turn, that increased satisfaction gives you more energy. It's a virtuous cycle.'[1]

What you really want

Once again, we can support these ideas with science. Fortunately for humankind, there are a whole lot of research psychologists working on a branch of their subject called the psychology of wellbeing. These researchers have chosen to spend their entire careers trying to figure out what people really want: what really makes them happy and what motivates them. One prominent set of ideas, Self Determination Theory (SDT), was pioneered by Edward Deci and Richard Ryan from the University of Rochester, New York, over 30 years ago, and now has a good deal of international recognition. (For more about this see Deci and Flaste, 1995.)

---

[1] Exclusive discussion with Patrick Quinlan, April 2008.

This theory states that there are three basic needs that foster psychological growth: **competence**, **relatedness**, and **autonomy**. They are defined as follows:

- **Competence** is the need to feel effective. A feeling of competence is developed through optimal challenge – that is, by doing things that are possible but not too easy – and by receiving supportive and sincere feedback.

- **Relatedness** is meaningful connection with other people. A feeling of relatedness is gained from warmth, caring, and a sense of significance.

- **Autonomy** is a feeling of volition, of being in control of one's direction. Autonomy is maximised as one is increasingly able to make decisions in the absence of either internal or external coercion.

When all three of these needs are met, an individual achieves satisfaction. When only one is thwarted, the individual becomes frustrated and finds ways of compensating.

An important feature of SDT is the way competence, relatedness, and autonomy interplay with two distinct forms of motivation: **intrinsic** and **extrinsic** motivation. You have the first of these when you do something because you like doing it, and not because of the expected consequences. This is pretty much what children do when they play. They do it for the pleasure of playing and with no ulterior purpose.

Extrinsic motivation, on the other hand, is when you do something as a means to an end. This is true when you do something to please somebody or to avoid being punished, and it's also true when you do something to meet a personal objective. In the latter case, even though you're performing the act for yourself, you're doing it as a means to an end. So, for example, if you perform a task either because somebody coerced you into doing it or because you see it as a way of making a lot of money, your motivation is said to be extrinsic. In either of these two cases, your sense of autonomy is diminished.

Researchers have collected an enormous amount of evidence to support the conclusion that we are most productive when we're intrinsically motivated. In this case, we are autonomous – there is no ulterior motive, and no pressure on us to make certain choices or perform certain actions. The problem with this finding is that it seems to indicate that we can only do our best when the task itself is pleasurable. Unfortunately, not all tasks come that way – sometimes we need to do things as a means to an end.

TIP #9

The more you feel a sense of choice in what you do, the better you'll do it.

The good news is that running a close second to intrinsic motivation is something called **self-regulated extrinsic motivation**. Now, that sounds complicated, but what it boils down to is this. When you perform a task for reasons other than the intrinsic pleasure of the activity, you can regulate the way you accept it. The process of accepting such a task is called internalisation. The more you remain autonomous as you internalise the idea coming from the outside, the better you integrate it into your own personal value system, and the more effectively you will perform the task.

The worst case is where you see no value in the activity, but you do it because you are coerced into doing it. In this case you may comply, but with resentment – and there's a good chance that you'll eventually act in defiance. The second-to-worst case is when you attach your ego to an activity or you perform the activity to avoid a feeling of guilt. When you perform a task to bolster your pride or to chase away guilt, you have introjected the values associated with the task. **Introjection** is like swallowing values without really digesting them. Much better is the case where you personally accept the importance of the task – a process called **identification**. And, finally, the best form of internalisation is **integration**, whereby the value system has been brought into congruence with your own values and needs.

Integration is still a form of extrinsic motivation, because you are still doing something for the sake of outcomes that are separate from the intrinsic enjoyment of the task itself. However, you remain autonomous in choosing to perform the task. Because your need for autonomy is met, your wellbeing is not threatened.

> Former CEO of Stewart Enterprises (a global company specialising in death care products and services), Frank Stewart knows all too well that time runs out.
>
> Frank says the biggest factors in being productive are involving yourself in a vocation you love and having good feelings towards the people you work with.

Now let's turn our attention to what psychologists have to say about happiness or wellbeing. Researchers make the distinction between two general kinds of wellbeing: **hedonic** and **eudaimonic** wellbeing. The first is a question of pleasure attainment and pain avoidance; the second is derived from having a meaningful existence and achieving self-actualisation. The difference between the two is similar to the difference between fun and satisfaction.

Researchers conduct experiments to try and find out the degree to which different events or situations make people happy. These experiments measure 'subjective happiness' in a number of ways. One commonly used benchmark is the number of people who respond 'very happy' to a question periodically posed in the National Opinion Research Center's 'General Social Survey of Americans'. The question is 'Taken all together, how would you say things are these days – would you say you are very happy, pretty happy, or not too happy?'

Out of all of these studies comes a finding that won't surprise you if you believe all the fables you heard in your childhood: it turns out that money really doesn't make you happy. Psychologist David Myers has developed a graph that demonstrates this. His graph, seen in Figure 4.1, shows the subjective happiness of the average American over time against the buying power of the average American over the same period. Other research has found that people living in the slums of Calcutta are more satisfied than one might expect (Biswas-Diener and Diener 2001).

Figure 4.1 Subjective happiness and personal income (from davidmyers.org)

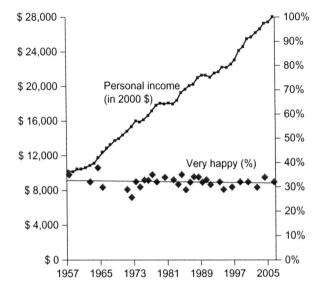

Still other experiments have shown that people who become blind or paralysed usually recover near-normal levels of day-to-day happiness (Gerhart et al. 1994; Myers 1993). The transition period is certainly hard, but once people adjust their expectations, they seem to snap right back to approximately the same level of subjective happiness as before.

What about money as a reward or as incentive? Surprisingly some of the experiments carried out by Deci and colleagues have shown that money as a reward is slightly demotivating. Competence, relatedness, and autonomy are what we're really after. When money is offered to perform a task, the subject feels seduced or even coerced. Even if the subject wanted to carry out that task in the first place, when a monetary reward is offered this feeling of autonomy is undermined. Performance dips.

I certainly don't want to be misinterpreted as saying that you should try to get less money. On the contrary, you should strive to get as much as the market will give you for what you do. But be cognisant of the fact that when you get too focused on money and feel seduced by it, you are likely to be less effective. When we strive for satisfaction we are at our best. If, on the way to satisfaction, we are lucky enough to be able to do things that are intrinsically pleasurable, we can do even better.

Armed with these findings from cognitive psychologists, I asked some of the CEOs what motivates them. The response I got from the president of Tulane University sums it up nicely. Scott Cowen said: 'Nobody does these jobs just for the financial compensation, especially not the job of running a university. I'm not sure if I would use the word 'fun'; 'satisfaction' is a better word to describe the personal benefit I get from my job. I do get a great deal of satisfaction.'

'I frequently ask myself if there is another job I can do where I would feel like I'm making a greater contribution to society. I'm not sure I would get that feeling if I were a corporate CEO,' Scott said. 'I might. But I definitely feel that way running a university.'

'To me it's a very noble thing to do,' he said. 'You get very high levels of satisfaction, and you feel like you're really making a difference. That's very rewarding, and that is what allows you to spend all the hours doing what you have to do. You remember in the end you are making a difference.'[2]

MANAGING YOUR ATTITUDE

Attitude is one of the important things that separate those who get a lot done from those who go through life frustrated. The assumptions you make about the world around you – and your motivation for doing things – have an impact on how much you get done and the quality of what you do. You can manage your attitude to some extent by rethinking your assumptions about a given situation. And where rethinking your assumptions doesn't cause a change, at least you can be aware of where your attitude is an impediment, and compensate accordingly. Let's have a closer look.

---

[2] Exclusive discussion with Scott Cowen, March 2008.

Keeping your cool

The first thing to review is how you react in tense situations. Exploding in the face of conflict diverts attention from the problem at hand. It has a destructive effect on relationships, thereby creating new problems. On the other hand, if you can keep a cool head, you'll find you can resolve the conflict much more quickly. In many cases you can enhance relationships by working through the challenging experience together.

To find out more about this, I talked to Jim Holbrook. Anybody who's ever met Jim is likely to notice that he's almost always in a good mood. It doesn't appear that his good nature has hurt his career. After all, Jim has held several senior positions in Ralston Purina and Procter & Gamble. Following that, he became CEO of Zipatoni, and now he is CEO of EMAK, a publicly traded company providing marketing services. I don't mean to suggest that people can will themselves into having such a good nature. But I think Jim might have some things to tell us about keeping a level head in the face of diversity.

Jim told me: 'I seldom get angry. My desire is to stay upbeat all the time. This doesn't make me a pushover. I still state my opinion and make tough decisions. I know that some people think if you stay positive and respect people you can't get what you want. That's a myth.'

'The way you say things, or the attitude you convey, is different from the content of what you say,' according to Jim. 'These are really two separate dimensions. The first has to do with maintaining good personal relationships. The second has to do with passing a message: expressing a need, an opinion, or what have you. If you stay positive you can maintain good relationships – even if the actual message is tough.'

TIP #10

If you keep your cool in the face of diversity, you'll save time in the long run.

Jim summed it up: 'There's really very little you can't communicate in an upbeat manner.'[3]

It's safe to say that Richard Branson would agree. In his autobiography he says he can count on the fingers of one hand the number of times he has lost his temper. (Branson 2004) This hasn't stopped him from starting and running several multinational companies in different industries and making revenue in the billions of dollars. On the contrary, it's probably helped him build good relationships, which have benefited him immensely over the years.

The pitfalls of perfectionism

You should strive for perfection but recognise that you'll rarely achieve it. When you finish something that falls short of perfection, don't sit around agonising in hindsight about all the flaws in your approach. Take mistakes into account and think about how you can improve, but don't torture yourself over your past failings. Just keep on moving forward.

You have to make decisions based on the information you have, and you have to accept tradeoffs. The important thing is to move forward.

When I asked Patrick Quinlan about perfectionism he said: 'You can't fight a battle without casualties. It isn't that you should be indifferent to the cost. But you have to accept that if you want to achieve something, you're going to incur a cost. If you try to achieve something without accepting cost, you probably won't get very far. You have to be very comfortable, deep inside, with tradeoffs. But you should be clear about what they are, so there are no surprises.'

'You're never going to get it right all the way, but you can at least do the things that are important. That's how we make real progress. It's embarrassingly simple,' Pat told me.

Continuing on that thought, he said: 'There is a vast difference between a mentality of perfectionism versus a mentality of

---

[3] Exclusive discussion with Jim Holbrook, March 2008.

improvement. In the first case you think everything is obtainable, which means you will ultimately fail. Then you accept that you are part of that failure, or you might choose to blame others. Neither of these is particularly constructive. Each tends to create a cycle of blame and denial, thereby taking away from working on the problems at hand. When you get into a finger-pointing mentality, you start to portray yourself better than what you are, and the other person or people worse than what they are. That whole cycle tends to take on a life of its own. The result is a culture that is not supportive, and one lacking in mutual respect.'

Pat went on: 'Whereas, if you have a mentality of improvement you are saying we know we are fallible – and we can never achieve perfection – but we can make improvements. There are things we understand and things we don't. There are things within our control and things outside our control. So we can't influence the whole spectrum. But we can still work to make improvements in areas we can influence. This kind of thinking tends to be much more uplifting. And it tends to bring people together – especially if the attitude is discussed openly.'[4]

Choosing to be present

Some people seem to be doing a million things at once. Take, for example, Charlice Byrd. As House Representative in Georgia, Charlice has to look after constituents, she has to work with businesses, she has to stay on top of what's going on in her state and in the rest of the country, and she has to work with other representatives. Not only is she a state representative; Charlice also serves on several committees and on the boards of directors of several non-profit organisations. In some cases she's head of the committee or organisation.

TIP #11

Always focus on the task at hand – especially when you're dealing with people.

---

[4] Exclusive discussion with Patrick Quinlan, April 2008.

I couldn't figure out how she managed to do so much at once, so I went and asked her. Much to my surprise, I found out that Charlice does not do very much at once. In fact, she only does one thing at a time. 'Whatever is in front of you at the moment is what you have to focus on,' she told me. 'Choose to be present. The best you can do is one thing at a time. If you try to do more than that, you'll wind up doing less. When you deal with people, especially, give that person your full attention.'[5]

We'll talk more about the downside of multitasking later in the book. For now, let's see what some of the business leaders have to say about doing whatever is in front of you – about choosing to be present.

Frank Stewart of Stewart Enterprises says: 'Always focus on the task at hand. If you're with somebody on the phone, do only that. Be there in the conversation. If you're in a meeting, be present. If you're doing a task by yourself, focus on that. If you're going to sleep, sleep. Don't think about all the things you did during the day, or about what you are going to do tomorrow. Don't try to solve problems. Sleep.'

Herb Kelleher did such a spectacular job of running Southwest Airlines that he managed to make a profit when very few competitors could. He stays focused on what's in front of him – and he especially does this when he's dealing with people.

Pay attention to the person you're talking with. If you're thinking about something else, you lose in three ways: you don't advance whatever it is that's distracting you, you don't get much out of the conversation, and you insult the person in front of you because they can tell you're not listening. (*Fortune* 2005)

'It takes some discipline and self-confidence to focus just on the task at hand,' Frank told me. 'You have to reach a point where you know you can face challenges as they come, so you don't have to think about them all at once.'

---

[5] Exclusive discussion with Charlice Byrd, May 2008.

When you're dealing with other people, being present is even more important. Not only is there an exchange of information with people that requires your attention to catch all of the important details, but there is also the emotional or relationship-building element of all human exchanges. If people don't feel you're listening to them, you may lose their interest and thereby miss out on a potentially valuable relationship.

Frank Stewart said: 'When you're dealing with people, you can't think of time management in the same way. Give them your full attention and don't look at your watch.'[6]

What prevents us from being present? Most people have dozens of goals at any given time. Sometimes we think we have to keep those in mind or we'll forget them. One way to overcome this is to make it a habit to write down your goals and consult your list at regular intervals.

Another thing that prevents us from focusing on the task at hand is that we sometimes waste mental energy agonising over something we didn't do. This could be something we didn't finish in the way we wanted, or it could be something we chose not to do. By learning to make clean stopping points on a given activity and learning to detach yourself emotionally after turning things down, you can free your mind of some of this clutter.

Finally, it's hard to be present when you are constantly interrupted. Sometimes this is beyond your control, but often it's not. Make it a habit to block off time for focused effort. If you can get used to thinking about just one thing for an hour or so every day, you'll develop your ability to concentrate – a capacity that will serve you well at other times.

We'll address all of these techniques later in the book. For now, give some thought to why it's sometimes hard to focus on what's in front of you.

Expectations versus goals
One more important aspect of attitude is what you expect. Ray Titus told me: 'My company helps many people start a business.

---

[6] Exclusive discussion with Frank Stewart, April 2008.

I've observed that if when you start out you spend a lot of time thinking about what you'll do if you fail – if you think about how you're going to file bankruptcy – you're going to fail. The people who start out saying things like "I'm going to be your biggest operation" are the ones who succeed.'

The CEO of United Franchise Group went on to say: 'Usually I can tell which franchisees are going to be the top producers and those who are going to fail. This is based on their attitude – the kinds of questions they have. This tells me whether they think they deserve success and whether they understand they'll have to give to get. It's inevitable.'

'What you believe is going to happen is going to happen,' Ray summarised. 'It's basic. If you go up to bat thinking you're going to strike out, you probably will. If you go up thinking you'll win the game, you'll probably do well.'[7]

The lesson here is that you can set a goal to achieve something, but even more powerful is **expecting** to achieve it. Think of getting what you want as part of the normal course of events.

THE ECONOMICS OF AUTHENTICITY

When I asked Dan Packer what he thinks makes the difference between somebody who gets a lot done and somebody who doesn't, he started out by saying: 'I think it all boils down to internal attitude. That's not the same thing as external attitude, which is what you display to other people. I think we lie to ourselves all the time about something that we think we want to do, even though we get this feeling in our gut telling us we don't really want to do it. We typically fool ourselves.'

'If you listen to it,' Dan said, 'your internal attitude will drive you. If you tune in to it, things run a lot smoother. I don't think anybody listens to it one hundred percent of the time, but the people who get closest to that are the most effective.'[8]

---

[7] Exclusive discussion with Ray Titus, July 2008.
[8] Exclusive discussion with Dan Packer, October 2008.

Honesty and sincerity

During my first discussion with John Dane about some of the best things you can do to get the most out of your time, we quickly got on to the subject of dealing with people. The CEO of Trinity Yachts jumped immediately to the crux of the matter: 'I cannot overemphasise the importance of being honest and fair with people. Simply for selfish reasons, it's what you have to do. If you have a habit of lying, people will pick up on that.'[9]

Another selfish reason for not lying is that it simply takes too much time. As Louis Kincannon, former director of the US Census Bureau, says, 'It's much more difficult to tell a web of half-truths than it is just to tell the truth. Obviously there are things you can't say with complete clarity, but as a rule of thumb, the closer you are to telling the truth, the easier it is to remember what you said.'[10]

Sometimes telling the truth means telling people what they don't want to hear, but you have to accept short-term discomfort to reap long-term benefits. Scott Cowen put it this way: 'One of the key principles of using your time well is being candid and direct with people. That's a lesson we all have to learn. That doesn't mean you are curt or rude. Somebody might come in with an idea they love. If you don't like the idea and know you can't support it, you have to tell that person right away. Or you may have one or two things you don't like about the idea. You have to tell the other person in clear terms what it is you have concerns with and what they have to do so that you will even consider supporting it.'

'I think directness in conversation, openness, and transparency are very important,' Scott said. 'It goes along with the ability to say "no" to people. You have to be able to say "yes", "no", or "maybe" in clear terms. When it's "maybe" you have to be very clear about where the doubt is and what has to happen for you to move from "maybe" to "yes". A lot of people don't like conflict. So they won't be clear. It's hard to do, but it's the best thing to do, because it's not misleading.'[11]

---

[9] Exclusive discussion with John Dane III, March 2008.
[10] Exclusive discussion with Louis Kincannon, May 2008.
[11] Exclusive discussion with Scott Cowen, March 2008.

TIP #12

Tell people what you really think. You won't have to spend time backtracking, and you'll build credibility, which will pay dividends in the long run.

Dan Packer said that you need to develop trust with people over time. This means telling people what you know when it affects them. 'The worst thing that can happen is that some point in the future, the person thinks: "That son of a gun knew some things and he didn't tell me." You don't want that. Get it all out on the table and let them know what you know.'

'The worst thing you can do is be manipulative,' Dan said. 'People pick up on that and sometimes they resent it more than being lied to.'

Dan brought his point home: 'Morals and ethics aside, lying is simply not efficient. Lying to others is not; nor is lying to yourself. There are at least two reasons it's expensive to lie. First, to be consistent in your lies, you have to construct a parallel reality and communicate that reality in a coherent manner. Second, when people start to suspect you're lying, your credibility is diminished, and from then on there is an element of doubt in all communications between you and that person. For both these reasons, in the long run, lying turns out to be a big time waster.'[12]

Similarly, former commandant of the US Coast Guard James Loy told me: 'Honesty builds credibility. When you lose credibility you lose out on fruitful relationships. Honesty builds bonds and therefore provides the basis for effective teamwork. For these reasons alone, being honest is a good use of your time.'[13]

Authenticity
Beyond honesty and sincerity is authenticity. For a good definition of authenticity, we can listen to what British psychoanalyst

---

[12] Exclusive discussion with Dan Packer, October 2008.
[13] Exclusive discussion with James Loy, May 2008.

Donald Winnicott had to say on the subject. In much of his writing he made the distinction between **true self** and **false self**. The true self is the instinctive core of the personality that can be creative and can feel real. The false self, on the other hand, is the persona one takes on to comply with external rules. Even with the appearance of success to the outside world and to oneself, when the false self has the upper hand, there is a feeling of unreality – a sense of not really being alive.

When you're authentic – or, as Winnicott puts it, when your true self is involved – you are honest with yourself. You do yourself the favour of going after what you really want. You eliminate all the unnecessary behaviour required to hide the truth from yourself and others. (See Winnicott 2005 for more about this.)

On this subject Patrick Quinlan told me: 'Being authentic is simply the most efficient way of conducting your life. And it's sustainable. You'll probably never completely know who you really are, but the closer you get to that, the better. It takes a lot of introspection, but it's really the only way to go through life.'[14]

I asked Manny Perez de la Mesa about being authentic. He's the CEO of the Fortune 1000 company PoolCorp, a worldwide leader in selling swimming pool equipment. Manny had this to say: 'It might cause some uneasiness in the short term, but the more you know who you really are, the better you communicate that to others. Consequently, you and others will experience less overall discomfort in the long run. You have to take a close look in the mirror sometimes and face things that are tough to face.'

Manny said: 'Once you know who you really are, you have to make sure others know as well. For example, saying "no" might be hard, but it's usually much cheaper for all involved. If you're true to yourself, you'll know when you don't like something or can't support something. You have to make sure others know that – and you have to let them know as soon as you can.'[15]

---

[14] Exclusive discussion with Patrick Quinlan, April 2008.
[15] Exclusive discussion with Manny Perez de la Mesa, March 2008.

THE IMPORTANCE OF PEOPLE

Think of human achievement – the legal infrastructures, the constitutional governments, the great advances in medicine, the development of microprocessors, the space exploration, and the construction of thousands of miles of highway systems. Think of all the great leaps forward. All that was accomplished without your presence or assistance, and yet you are one of the beneficiaries. Billions of people have done the right things without you. Humbling? It sure is. This fact also serves as a reminder of how much we rely on other people.

Almost everything you do involves acquiring something from somebody or passing something on to somebody. How you take things and how you give them are essential. If you do something for somebody else without handing it off in the right way – for example, if the other person does not perceive the value – you may have wasted your time doing it in the first place.

Charlice Byrd put it this way: 'Let's face it; no person is an island. No matter what you do, it's going to involve people. You might as well brush up on your people skills – and when you do, you'll find it pays back in many ways. Once you start to listen to other people – and really understand them – you're surprised at how much satisfaction you get from the emotional bond. Not only that; you learn a lot from that other person, and that other person will help you in ways you didn't expect.'

Charlice explained: 'You may think you get things done by yourself. In fact, there is very little you can accomplish without other people being involved. If you're successful, it's because other people have helped elevate you to success.'[16]

> **TIP #13**
>
> There's very little that you can accomplish without the help of other people. Get good at dealing with people.

---

[16] Exclusive discussion with Charlice Byrd, May 2008.

It follows that a key element of time management is to surround yourself with the right people. Try to get it right the first time around. But when you do make a mistake and invest a lot of time in someone it turns out you can't count on, face the problem. Admit you were wrong and start again.

Differing perception

Next time you are with somebody, take a few minutes to imagine switching places with that person. In this mind game, imagine that you are in exactly the same situation, but you are now that other person. Think of how differently you would see the interaction. The situation would seem as different as if you had transported yourself to another planet. Yet that person is right there with you.

Studies have been conducted in which people go into a meeting and afterwards independently report on what happened. It turns out there are big differences in what they report about the same meeting. This isn't surprising when one considers that the attendees are different in so many ways, including genetic makeup, gender, phases in biorhythm, memories, education, needs and agendas, and roles in the activity at hand.

You will never understand another person perfectly, but the most effective people never stop trying to get an idea of the differences between their own perception and that of other people. It's always valuable to try to home in on the underlying intentions of the other person. Too often when there is a misunderstanding, there is a tendency to think that the other person is acting maliciously. People do sometimes act maliciously, but that's relatively rare. Usually a misunderstanding is exactly that – a lack of understanding.

Respect

Admiral Loy had an extensive career with the US Coast Guard. He did everything from serving as a member of boarding parties to heading up that entire branch of the US military. 'I cannot overemphasise the importance of respecting other people,' he said. 'First of all, it's what people deserve. But also, purely from the standpoint of making the best use of your time, it's what you should do. If you respect people, they're more likely to go along with you. If you don't respect them, you'll encounter all sorts of resistance. And you have to do it all the time. If you can disrespect one person, then it becomes too easy for you to come up with a reason to disrespect someone else.'[17]

Former prime minister of Belize Manuel Esquivel has spent a lot of time working with people. Along the way, he must have learned a few things, so I asked him about the value of respecting other people. 'I guess it's a part of my personality, but I don't shout at people,' he told me. 'People know they are free to disagree. They know they can put forward another idea, and they're not wasting their time doing so. They know I will listen to what they have to say.'

TIP #14

Treat people with respect. It will help you build alliances and reduce your chances of developing a new enemy.

'People appreciate that, and they become more useful,' Manuel told me. 'They become more interested in solving problems rather than just waiting for me to tell them what to do. That saves me a lot of time, because it relieves me of the burden of having to do everything myself. They know it's worth their while to try to think of a really neat solution, because there's a good chance it will be accepted.'[18]

Trying to be liked by everybody
While the CEOs I talked to emphasised the importance of respecting other people, they didn't say you should try to be liked by everybody. Think about how ridiculous it is to try to be liked by everybody. What a waste of time.

Jim Whitehurst was Chief Operating Officer of Delta Airlines before going on to become CEO of Red Hat. On this subject he told me: 'Most people don't want to change and they don't want

---

[17] Exclusive discussion with James Loy, May 2008.
[18] Exclusive discussion with Manuel Esquivel, June 2008.

others around them to change. So if you are progressive, there will be people trying to stop you or slow you down. If you get frustrated by that, and get too focused on them, you become totally ineffective.'

'You need self confidence or some way of filtering this out,' Jim said. 'Otherwise, if you worry too much about what other people are thinking, chances are you'll let that drive your agenda. Good time management is not about just staying busy; it's more about choosing productive things to do. Generally worrying too much about what others are thinking or doing will prevent you from choosing the right things to do.'

'Obviously there are some key constituents, such as customers, the board of directors, investors, and the employee population as a whole,' he said. 'You have to work to win these people over. The point is a lot of people worry too much about peers or others around them whose opinion really does not matter in the long run. You have to get beyond that and follow your own compass. You need the self-confidence and the general sense that you are going in the right direction.'[19]

TIP #15

Don't let adverse opinions stand in your way. If you are doing something progressive, people will disagree with you. You have to move beyond this and do what you think is right.

Manuel Esquivel added: 'I've seen people who go out to dinner with somebody and have a laugh. They fool themselves into thinking that will mean the other person will then agree with just about anything. That's not at all the case. What's important to you may not be important to them. No matter how affable the relationship might have been, it will change when there's a conflict of interests.'

---

[19] Exclusive discussion with Jim Whitehurst, April 2008.

'When you can't agree, you just have to proceed,' he continued. 'It sounds simplistic, but in this case, you just have to do what you are convinced is the right thing to do, even if the other person thinks it's wrong. You have to make a decision in that way. You have to listen to what the other person has to say, but ultimately you're the one who has to draw the conclusion about what's the right thing to do. You have to be convinced.'[20]

Where you fit in

Struggling to make a success out of his student magazine in the early years, Richard Branson managed to get John Lennon to agree to an interview. But Lennon didn't show up. The unknown and very young Branson threatened to sue for losses incurred from the missed interview.

Richard Branson (2004) advises not letting yourself be intimidated, and not involving your ego when you're dealing with people. If you let your ego get involved, either you'll wind up feeling crushed by the other person or you'll wind up with an inflated view of yourself. Either way, you'll no longer think clearly.

When you sit down to negotiate, it's important to feel that you have just as much right to be at the negotiating table as anybody else there. You deserve just as much respect as the person on the other side.

If you go into a relationship thinking there is an imbalance between yourself and the other person, problems will occur. Either you'll think the other person is better and more deserving than you, or you'll think you are better and more deserving than him or her.

The best relationships are those based on mutual respect and where both parties are looking for win/win.

---

[20] Exclusive discussion with Manuel Esquivel, June 2008.

Communication

Patrick Quinlan, CEO of Ochsner Health Systems, said: 'I'm so fascinated by how people communicate. We have such different perspectives. We have different experiences, different assumptions, and different tastes that lead to different interpretations. I'm just amazed that we can do anything together at all. I wonder why people are surprised when it doesn't work. If you think about how much it takes for people to come together and share a view on a problem or on what needs to be done, there are just so many things that can go wrong.'

'What fools people is that we look alike, and therefore they conclude we are the same,' he said. 'Boy, we are not!'

According to Pat, 'One of the many departure points for misunderstanding is that you project your ideas onto other people. You have all these assumptions in your head and you think the other person thinks that way too.'[21]

The former director of the US Census Bureau, Louis Kincannon, told me: 'Just about anything you do in life involves receiving something from somebody else or giving something to somebody else. When you ask somebody for something, take the time to explain the intent and purpose of your request.'

He continued: 'And when you deliver something of value – a product or a service – to somebody else, it's also important to explain the purpose behind it. Make sure they know what they're getting and that they understand what it's for. It's like a finishing touch.'[22]

Thierry Grange had this to say: 'I spend a lot of time explaining decisions to people. Some people think I spend too much time doing this. But I think people do better work if they understand the purpose behind it, and why we choose one way of doing things as opposed to the alternatives. People need to know how what they do fits into the overall strategy.'[23]

---

[21] Exclusive discussion with Patrick Quinlan, April 2008.
[22] Exclusive discussion with Louis Kincannon, May 2008.
[23] Exclusive discussion with Thierry Grange, April 2008.

Maintain a consistent style and communicate it clearly

In almost every situation, you can save time by making it clear to people how to deal with you. If people understand your style, they know how to approach you and they know what to expect from you. Consequently interactions will be more effective and will be of greater benefit to both parties. To achieve this, you have to be consistent in how you deal with people – and you should do your best to communicate your style.

One way to accomplish this is to have a clear mission. Todd Davis says: 'When you have a mission, you project that to other people and they view you as consistent. They will pick up what your value system really is and they know not to bother you with things that are out of line with that.'[24]

President of the Consumer Business Unit at Symantec Janice Chaffin has naturally received a good deal of recognition, including being named one of the 'Top 100 Women in Corporate America' by *Women 3.0 Magazine*.

Janice says it's important to be consistent and to make sure others understand your style. Respect them and make it clear you respect them. Everything runs a whole lot more smoothly when people know how to approach you, and when they know they will be treated with respect.

As we discussed before, respecting people goes a long way, and so does letting people discover that you will respect them. 'It's really important to be consistent in your management style – and to clearly signal that style to people,' Janice Chaffin told me. 'If people know what kind of information you're looking for before being able to say "yes" or "no", that makes things run much smoother. It's also important to respect people and for people to know you will respect them. Not only is this the decent thing to do; it's also the efficient thing to do. When people feel they can come to you and be respected, they will be more honest. I can't think of any business where it's not important for management

---

[24] Exclusive discussion with Todd Davis, March 2008.

to know what's really going on. Make it easy for people to keep you in the know.'

'This is true in business and it's true in life,' Janice said. 'Maintain a consistent style and treat people with dignity. Anything you do to develop this will be a good use of your time. In the long run you will reap big benefits.'[25]

Not only is consistency important for organisations; it's also important for individuals. Steve Hansel told me: 'Great companies share a consistency of vision and a consistency of purpose that comes from really understanding what it is they are trying to do and communicating that clearly throughout the company. If people understand the values of the company, they can more easily make decisions about how to deal with specific situations. If they understand the priorities of the company, that helps them be efficient with their time. You might be in the banking business in Virginia and you say these are our markets, and by default, these other ones aren't. If somebody walks in off the street to ask for a loan to do something in California, you don't spend time with that person, because you don't operate in California. The point is you don't have to make decisions about a lot of things if you have a well-defined mission.'

According to Steve, 'A strategy that's well understood throughout the organisation helps people use their time efficiently. The same would be true for a customer service policy or a policy that deals with how to treat customers who have a financial problem with their loans. It's not so much about laying down a large book of rules as it is laying out a set of principles.'

'The same applies at the individual level,' Steve went on. 'Productive people have a consistent vision that they communicate to other people. They try hard not to be mysterious. This vision also helps guide the individual in making day-to-day decisions.'

Maintaining a consistent style and communicating it clearly is an important concept. Just as powerful is the idea of surrounding yourself with people you can count on – and making sure they can count on you, too.[26]

---

[25] Exclusive discussion with Janice Chaffin, March 2008.
[26] Exclusive discussion with Steve Hansel, March 2008.

THE POWER OF TRUST

Gary Heavin, the CEO of Curves, says: 'Two of the values I think are fundamental are honesty and integrity. Honesty is telling the truth the best you can, all the time. Integrity is doing what you say.'

According to Gary, 'With these principles in place, what people think of traditionally as time management comes naturally. Relationships based on trust are super efficient. Relationships that are stable, and that don't have to be revisited or rebuilt, are powerful. If you can develop relationships that are trusting and long lasting, can you imagine the time you save?'[27]

Counting on other people

Indeed, think of all the time wasted because you're not sure whether somebody really will do what they said they would do. When people can't be trusted, or when they're inconsistent and unreliable, dealing with them takes more time than it should. Conversely, when you interact with somebody you can count on, you don't have to spend time second guessing or checking up on that person.

> James Carter was president of Loyola University, New Orleans, for 27 years.
>
> He told me: 'Time spent determining who you hire is time very well spent, because you'll spend an awful lot of time picking up the mess if you make the wrong decision. Conversely, you'll reap big benefits for a long time if you hire the right person.'[28]

Supporting this point, the CEO of Energizer Holdings told me: 'If you have the right person who understands your expectations and where you need to go, and that person has a clear idea of how to get there, give him the freedom to do it, and you will get a good return. That takes a little bit of time up front, and it achieves a great result.'

---

[27] Exclusive discussion with Gary Heavin, April 2010.
[28] Exclusive discussion with James Carter, April 2008.

'At the other extreme,' Ward Klein continued, 'if you have somebody who is clueless, or is dysfunctional in some way, whether it be in people management or in ability to focus, you can spend a lot of time with that person and get poor results.'

One of the people he counts on most is his assistant. He explained: 'I rely on my executive assistant a great deal. Fortunately I have been blessed with a great one. The skill set includes knowing both on a business and a personal level what kinds of demands are on my time, what my priorities and game plan are, and being able to guide a lot of stuff that might not even hit my desk. She is a good gatekeeper. She's good at following up on details. If I need to go somewhere to see somebody or do something, I just need to say it and it happens. So there's a tremendous amount of time saving and efficiency thanks to having somebody I can count on and that I can trust.'[29]

Discussing this with the former CEO of Hibernia Corporation, Steve Hansel, I got this gem: 'I try to surround myself with people I can count on and whose skills complement my own. If you seek out people just like yourself, you'll inevitably have problems. If you try to control everything that happens and make every significant decision rather than delegating, you'll either drive yourself nuts or severely limit the size of your business, or both. So I think you have to surround yourself with reliable people who have skills that complement your own, and who share – within a reasonable tolerance – your vision of your place in the market and the strategic priorities and tactics that will take you from where you are to where you want to be.'[30]

TIP #16

Surround yourself with people you can count on and whose skills complement your own.

---

[29] Exclusive discussion with Ward Klein, March 2008.
[30] Exclusive discussion with Steve Hansel, March 2008.

Nick Mueller put it this way: 'You can't change other people, so you have to be careful who you invest time in. It's very much worth your while to invest in the right people. To make relationships or partnerships meaningful, you have to spend time working on them. You can never predict how they'll pay off, but they usually do pay off. It's like building bridges. You don't know ahead of time what kind of traffic they'll carry. Later on down the line, though, they will serve you in ways you didn't expect.'[31]

Clearly you need to be around people you can count on. What about how other people view you? What do the CEOs say about the importance of being somebody others can count on?

Making sure others can count on you
Successful companies and successful individuals know to deliver what they promise. They look for ways of helping the people most important to them. Not only is it a kind thing to do; it's also something that will give you a nice payback.

I discussed this point with the CEO of Trinity Yachts. 'When Hurricane Katrina hit, this building we're in was totally wiped out,' John Dane III said, referring to the building we were in while discussing time management. 'We had 550 employees the day Katrina hit. We now have over a thousand. Within two years after Katrina we not only recovered, but we doubled the company. We did that through a lot of hard work and by building loyalty and dedication.'

He told me: 'One of the things we were able to do after Katrina, as soon as we could get online, was to find all our employees' bank accounts and transfer $1500 to them. We realized that some of these people were living paycheck to paycheck and really needed the money. So we did what we could to help them out. And that was unbelievably appreciated by our people. That's why every one of the pre-Katrina employees who has come back to the area has come back to work for us.'

---

[31] Exclusive discussion with Gordon Mueller, April 2009.

John related how helping people in need was the right thing to do – it was satisfying to be able to make a difference in people's lives. But it also makes good business sense. It demonstrated to Trinity Yacht employees that they could count on him; and employees returned the favour through loyalty and hard work.[32]

Three hundred miles west, over in Brenham, Texas, just north of Houston, Paul Kruse agrees with the principle of making sure other people know they can count on you. He told me: 'Our success is due to collective effort. We have a lot of very talented people. If we lost those people, we couldn't do what we do. We have never laid anybody off. A lot of people like the security that provides, and they tend to stick around.'[33]

There's another Texan who has something to say on this. Gary Heavin and his wife, Diane, founded Curves and made it into the fastest-growing franchise company in history. He points out that people don't say nice things about you if you don't do what you say, and if they don't trust you.

'If, on the other hand, you value integrity, other people will see this,' Gary says. 'The efficiency of not having to prove yourself to someone over and over is extraordinary.'[34]

Building a team

Todd Davis, CEO of LifeLock, says: 'By building the right team around you, you can delegate the right pieces and know they will get done. I am not encumbered with the fear of not knowing what happened to something I handed off. I don't have to be bothered with checking up on things. I know it's going to get done. That is an advantage of being a CEO or managing a team. But you can also apply this idea to other situations where you're not managing a team. The underlying principle is to build relationships with people you can rely on.'[35]

---

[32] Exclusive discussion with John Dane III, March 2008.
[33] Exclusive discussion with Paul Kruse, March 2008.
[34] Exclusive discussion with Gary Heavin, April 2010.
[35] Exclusive discussion with Todd Davis, March 2008.

John Koerner started and ran Barq's Rootbeer, which was later bought by Coca Cola. He now runs Koerner Capital, an investment firm. In 2008 he was king of Mardi Gras in New Orleans.

John says different people are good at different things. It's important that people accept their personality type and try to surround themselves with personality types that complement their own. Everybody brings something of value to a team but in a unique way.

John Koerner told me: 'Each person brings his or her own skill sets. Some are good at the front end of the deal, and some are good at the back. Some are good at vision; some are good at detail. Some are proactive; some are reactive. You need all these things.'

'What's most important is that people realise what their personality type is, and don't try to be somebody they aren't,' John said. 'We have to recognise our strengths and weaknesses, and team with people who fill in for our shortcomings. The unifying forces for the team are the task or goal, recognition that everybody brings something different into the equation, and trust. Although teams form and reform quite often, if you bring a good history with you, you can establish a good team early. A good history would include a history of being trustworthy.'

John went on: 'To nurture a good team, you need to work together but also play together. You can establish good relationships outside the work environment. You can go fishing with them, go to a ball game with them, or have a drink with them. Much of the creativity flows from informal situations. Structured situations stifle free thought. A lot of great ideas come from free thinking.'[36]

James White told me about the importance of collaboration: 'I always make sure we have good cross-functional collaboration towards achieving goals. To this end, I pay careful attention to how well people are working together within a team and how well

---

[36] Exclusive discussion with John Koerner, June 2008.

different teams are working together. Collaboration requires trust, shared values, and common goals.'[37]

An important idea that came out of these discussions is that, strictly from a time management perspective, trust is a key element. If trust is present in both directions, you don't have to spend time second guessing other people, and they won't hesitate to send valuable information and ideas your way.

'WILL DO' GOALS

Now let's talk about setting goals. If you can set goals you are truly comfortable with, you're off to a good start. This is not to say it's a certainty you will reach these goals. Other things may come up that prevent you from accomplishing them, or your priorities might change. But at least you won't be personally conflicted with the course you've set.

To help with this, Master The Moment includes a technique called WILL DO. Set goals with the following traits, and you are sure to be motivated:

Within your control: You are not relying on external forces.

Important: The goal is significant.

Learning: Reaching the goal involves learning.

Love: The outcome is of benefit to other people.

Difficult: The work to reach the goal is challenging, but not impossible.

Optional: You don't have to accept this goal – you choose to.

Be careful not to trick yourself with this technique. That would be defeating the purpose. The idea is to modify your goals slightly so that your own involvement is defined differently. For example,

---

[37] Exclusive discussion with James White, April 2008.

instead of setting a goal 'to win ten deals next year', set a goal 'to do everything you possibly can to win ten deals next year'. There are three reasons why this makes a big difference. First, you don't waste any energy agonising over things beyond your control. Instead you focus on those things you yourself can do. Second, you have no excuses for not reaching this goal. Doing everything you can possibly do is only up to you – you alone are to blame if you don't reach it. Finally, if you don't win ten deals but you've done all you can possibly do, you've still reached your goal, and you can feel good about it. Remember there are all sorts of things beyond your control. You shouldn't agonise over them.

Make sure you spend your time doing things that are **important**. Not only should they be meaningful to you; they should also have a high impact.

You may start out with a goal for which you don't think you have anything to **learn**. If this is the case, rethink your goal. You don't want to get into the mindset that goal achievement is about demonstrating current capacity. Make sure you start out with a learning-oriented attitude. Furthermore, learning is intrinsically pleasurable, and can therefore make the work more satisfying and your performance higher.

Love should be involved. If you set out to do something only for selfish reasons, then maybe what you're striving for is not your best goal. Given that we only have a limited amount of time, think about doing things that benefit other people. You will achieve higher levels of satisfaction in accomplishing what you set out to do. What's more, you tend to perform better when doing something for the benefit of other people.

If a goal isn't **difficult**, it's not worth doing. Try to spend your time doing things that are challenging but not impossible. You'll feel much better about accomplishing them, and you'll be more motivated in working towards them.

Perhaps the most difficult part of a WILL DO goal is the last element – that it has to be **optional**. In many cases you feel as if you have to do something.

Let's go over this point with an example. Take the case of a boss you can't stand, who comes in and orders you to finish a project by the end of December. Don't make the mistake of making it your own goal to finish the project by the end of December. That's your 'mean' boss's goal.

Your goal is quite different. You can choose to look for another boss or to look for another job, or you might try to expose this boss. Alternatively you might seek to improve your relationship with him or her. Maybe there are some misunderstandings that can be cleared up. All of these are valid choices you can make.

In some cases completing the project by the end of December will be part of what you need to do to reach the goal you've chosen. In other cases it might not be. The point is to make your own choices.

HABITS

For one week, work on developing these two good habits.

Habit 1: Strive to be authentic
Striving to be authentic means being as honest with yourself as you can about what you want and why you do what you do. This doesn't mean you get to do everything you want to do. You'll always have obligations. Authenticity means being honest with yourself about your motivations.

Habit 2: Favour trusting relationships
You'll always have to deal with people you can't trust or people you know you can't count on, but you shouldn't put much energy into strengthening your relationships with these people. Instead put your efforts into building relationships with people you can trust and count on. Make sure those same people can trust and count on you.

How to work on habits
Here's the procedure to work on habits. In the morning think about the day's events that will allow you to reinforce these two habits. During the day take every opportunity to make them automatic. As a visual reminder, put this book, or a copy of this page, somewhere you can see it from time to time throughout the day. In the evening take five minutes to rate yourself on a scale of 1 to 5, with 1 indicating that you did very badly on the habit and 5 indicating that you did very well. Pencil in a rating for that day on the chart below.

HABIT	DAYS						
	1	2	3	4	5	6	7
Strive to be authentic.							
Favour trusting relationships.							

EXERCISES

As you did at the end of the first chapter, take the time to go through these exercises. Doing so will help you put the powerful ideas we discussed to work for you.

i   List the five things you spend most of your time doing. Now list five things you love doing – not because of any expected reward, but because the activity is intrinsically satisfying.

ii   Make a list of tasks you feel coerced into doing, whether it be a matter of external coercion (for example, from a threatening boss) or internal coercion (for example, because you'll feel guilty if you don't do them).

iii List things you're good at. List things you can get better at. List things that fall into neither category, but that could be of benefit to you. Look for people with these skills and with whom you can have a trusting relationship.

iv   Write down how other people perceive your style. Are you consistent? Are you approachable? Are there things you should change about your style? Think of what you can do to demonstrate to others that they can count on you.

v   Make a list of up to five WILL DO goals. Keep this list for exercises in subsequent chapters.

5 ENERGISE

It's amazing to see how much energy some people have. Take, for example, Daniel Doimo. He runs an organisation of thousands of people in more than 40 different countries and is responsible for revenue in the billions of dollars. Not only is Daniel himself energetic, but the company he runs is all about energy. APC by Schneider Electric sells uninterruptible power supplies, which kick in to provide juice to computers and other essential equipment whenever there's a power outage.

Daniel finds the time to work out for an hour and a half, two or three times a week. Perhaps it's more accurate to say that he **makes** the time to work out, because he knows working out pays dividends. According to Daniel, 'To manage a large multi-national organisation, you have to be in top shape physically, mentally, and spiritually.' He advises anybody trying to become more effective to 'take time for yourself and take care of yourself. This is one of those cases where you need to slow down to go faster. If you're at the top of your game, you can get a lot more done.'[1]

CEO of CCI Systems John Jamar is also a triathlete. Ten years ago he was not in very good shape. Now he is. Because he's physically fit, he's on task all day long.

John says: 'There is no question that when people are healthy they're engaged and energetic. They think clearly. When you're in great physical shape you sleep well at night, so when you're in the office you get through the day with more energy. Being out of shape is a huge disadvantage, even if you're just doing brain work.'[2]

Daniel doesn't stand alone. Virtually every CEO I talked with made a point of telling me how important they think it is to stay in shape. Patrick Quinlan expounded on how being physically fit increases your attention span and your ability to contribute. He said: 'Fitness has to do with energy. It's one thing to attend – it's another to really contribute. For this reason I would recommend to anybody who wants to accomplish much to take very good care of their physical health. That means getting exercise, eating properly, and getting enough rest. You should monitor yourself like an athlete would.'

Pat told me he likes to draw the analogy with a baseball pitcher. 'Pitchers sit in the bull pen to rest their arms,' he said. 'You can only pitch so many innings, and after a while you're not very good

---

[1] Exclusive discussion with Daniel Doimo, March 2008.
[2] Exclusive discussion with John Jamar, March 2008.

any more. Like any athlete, you need to know your limits and respect them. You can easily gloss over this point. I think it's very important, because not only does it have to do with your energy, but also with your mental health. Your mental and physical health are often intertwined.'

'This is one area where the average person gives little thought,' he explained. 'It really does affect performance, and this is what we're talking about here: performance. Most of us have around 120 waking hours per week. Are those really productive hours, or are those hours where you're just attending?'[3]

EXERCISE

Practically all the CEOs I talked with exercise several times a week. For example, the CEO of American Reprographics, K. Suriyakumar (Suri), leaves the office to work out for an hour during the middle of the day. 'I cannot miss my exercise, because it's critical to my wellbeing,' he says.[4]

The Chancellor of the University of Maryland agrees. Brit Kirwan said: 'I usually average two or three times a week. I try to make my exercise something around tennis, whether it be to hit against a backboard, or a match against somebody else. I find tennis a very good form of exercise. It's aerobic and you use most parts of your body. I have a lot of energy – I feel that way and others have shared with me the observation that they find me energetic. Throughout my life I have exercised on a regular basis, and I find this contributes a great deal to my energy level.'[5]

Benefits of exercise

What the CEOs say about exercise is consistent with what scientific studies have shown. According to research published in *American Family Physician* (Saeed, Antonacci and Bloch, 2010), exercise improves your mood and helps you sleep better. The American College of Sports Medicine (Pollock et al. 1998) says that exercise contributes positively to your energy level. It does so directly by increasing

---

[3] Exclusive discussion with Patrick Quinlan, April 2008.
[4] Exclusive discussion with K. Surivakumar, March 2008.
[5] Exclusive discussion with William Kirwan, March 2008.

oxygen flow through improved circulation, and indirectly by helping you sleep, which in turn gives you more energy.

As for the President's Council on Physical Fitness, they report that there is a good deal of evidence showing a relationship between exercise and improved mental health (Rankinen and Bouchard 2002). Exercise reduces anxiety and depression and it appears to bring about positive mood states and enhanced self-esteem. Evidence also indicates that intellectual ability is enhanced through exercise. While nobody know exactly how this works, one plausible explanation would be that your brain functions better as a result of increased oxygen flow. This and improvements in mood, also brought on by regular exercise, probably enhance intellectual performance.

Ward Klein rose through the ranks to become CEO of Energizer Holdings. He exercises at least three days a week for an hour and a half at a time.

Ward says he's much more productive on the afternoons after he's worked out. That's one of the reasons he makes exercise a priority.[6]

With those words on what the medical community is saying about exercise, let's go back and see what some of the other CEOs say about the benefits of working out.

Let's start with the CEO of Porter Novelli. Gary Stockman says: 'Exercise has huge benefits for me personally. I try to exercise every day for about 45 minutes. I try to work it in even when I'm traveling. I'm a morning exerciser, which is good, because that way I have more control over whether it happens or not.'

According to Gary, 'Time spent exercising pays off in spades throughout a work day. I'm more effective and more energetic. Until you make it a real habit you have a sort of negotiation

---

[6] Exclusive discussion with Ward Klein, March 2008.

with yourself: "Am I going to do it or should I just lay in bed?" At first it can be difficult, but it gets easier over time, because you know what the answer is going to be. The answer is that you are going to do it, so there is no point in debating.'[7]

The CEO of Red Hat told me he does his best to work out four or five days a week. 'I feel the difference,' Jim Whitehurst said. 'On the days I don't work out, I don't feel as good as on the days I do work out. Even getting on the exercise bike for just a half hour makes a big difference for me. If your body isn't running right you aren't going to be effective. Your brain works so much better if your blood is flowing.'[8]

Cardiovascular training

Not only do the CEOs like to exercise; several of the ones I talked with are marathon runners. For example, Jim Holbrook of EMAK just recently completed his first one. He said training for the marathon helped his attitude. Jim already has a great attitude naturally; it's noteworthy that he still looks for ways of improving it.[9]

TIP #17

Make exercise a priority. You'll enjoy a high return on the time you invest in exercise.

The CEO of Redknee, Lucas Skoczkowski, also runs marathons. 'In January 2005 I decided to start running to increase my general efficiency,' he said. 'That was a New Year's resolution. In May that year I did my first half marathon. In October I ran my first full marathon. Now I run half marathons and full marathons from time to time.'[10]

You don't have to be a marathon runner to get a cardiovascular workout. For some people simply walking several times a week does the trick. Take, for example, James Carter, a Jesuit priest

---

[7] Exclusive discussion with Gary Stockman, March 2008.
[8] Exclusive discussion with Jim Whitehurst, April 2008.
[9] Exclusive discussion with Jim Holbrook, March 2008.
[10] Exclusive discussion with Lucas Skoczkowski, April 2008.

and former president of Loyola University in New Orleans. During his 25-year term heading up the university, he walked every morning. 'I would take a brisk walk for around 35 minutes. That's exactly how long it takes me to make my way around Audubon park just across the street from Loyola. I always felt that was my contribution to people I worked with. It put me in a better mood, and it made me more energetic. Exercise saves you time in the long run. On top of that, exercise time is time you subconsciously work on some of your big problems.'

Exercise provides such good 'think time' that Father Carter still does his sermon preparation while engaging in a light workout. 'Exercise has several benefits,' he summarises. 'The physical benefits include raised energy levels. The psychological benefits include better attitude. A nice by-product is that it gives you time and a good mental state to think things through.'[11]

Frequency of exercise

As for how often to exercise, the American College of Sports Medicine (Pollock et al. 1998) says that a good training programme should include 20 to 60 minutes of aerobic exercise, three to five days per week. The daily exercise can be continuous or it can be intermittent with each session lasting at least 10 minutes. The absolute minimum, therefore, would be to perform two 10-minute sessions of aerobic exercise on three different days every week.

If you're not yet convinced that exercise is an essential part of time management, consider this. If you put in three hours a week exercising, you're using around two-and-a-half per cent of your waking hours. Suppose this routine makes you ten per cent more effective. That's an excellent return.

NUTRITION

TIP #18

Eat a light lunch and drink water throughout the day. Doing so will help you maintain the energy you need to do the things you want.

---

[11] Exclusive discussion with James Carter, April 2008.

Not surprisingly, almost all the CEOs I talked with are careful about what they eat. As James White of Jamba Juice said, 'What you put in largely determines your energy level and your output.'[12] Elaborating on this, Daniel Doimo told me: 'I watch what I eat. I have a very balanced diet. I rarely drink. When I do, I don't have more than two or three glasses of wine. I don't smoke.'[13] Similarly, Brit Kirwan offers: 'I am very conscious about what I eat. I don't eat many sweets or high-calorie foods.'[14]

What's important is that you develop eating habits that work for you. 'I don't eat breakfast,' said Ward Klein. 'I eat a very light lunch after working out. Then I eat dinner. This may not be exactly what most people say are healthy eating habits, but it seems to work for me. I absolutely do think about eating right.'[15]

'I am meticulous about my diet,' Jim Whitehurst said. 'I eat virtually no simple carbs. I eat oatmeal or fruit for complex carbs, but simple carbs make you feel good for about an hour and then you crash hard. I always eat breakfast. If I don't, I get a midday lull. My breakfast is either low carb or complex carb. If you have the average American diet with lots of simple carbs and simple sugars, your body is on a roller coaster through the day. There's no way your brain can be effective under those conditions.'[16]

Gilles du Chaffaut is director of city services for the city of Grenoble, France. He's the one who makes sure the city is running – and he has 3000 people working for him to help get the job done.

He says: 'Eating a big lunch will slow you down so much it may ruin your afternoon. Living in France, I have to be especially careful at lunchtime.'[17]

---

[12] Exclusive discussion with James White, April 2008.
[13] Exclusive discussion with Daniel Doimo, March 2008.
[14] Exclusive discussion with William Kirwan, May 2008.
[15] Exclusive discussion with Ward Klein, March 2008.
[16] Exclusive discussion with Jim Whitehurst, April 2008.
[17] Exclusive discussion with Gilles du Chaffaut, November 2008.

Similarly, John Jamar told me: 'I try to stay away from simple carbohydrates. I get my carbs from fruits and vegetables.'[18]

On what it takes to keep your energy up, Ray Titus, the head of United Franchise Group, told me: 'I think it's really important to drink lots of water. That's something not many people think about. I keep five water coolers around the office. In every office in America, people drink a lot of coffee in the morning. It might help them do what they have to do in the morning, but after lunchtime they plunge. It's obvious why. You have to get water in your system. For this reason, we encourage people to drink a lot of water. We even go so far as to pass out water bottles during the day.'[19]

SLEEP

Some people think that, with all the responsibility that comes with the job, CEOs don't sleep well. That seems not to be true. Almost all the CEOs I talked to said they slept very well at night.

Brit Kirwan is chancellor of the University System of Maryland. He is responsible for 13 institutions, with a staff of around 25,000 and a budget of around $3.5 billion. Brit goes to bed between 11 p.m. and midnight and gets up at around five or five thirty. 'I never take a nap,' he said, 'not even on the weekend. I can't remember the last time I took a nap.'[20]

Lucas Skoczkowski said: 'I sleep well. If I don't sleep enough, I'll fall asleep – anywhere and at any time. My body simply shuts down. The optimal amount of sleep for me is around six hours. If I only get four hours, that's not enough. I travel in quite a few timezones. No matter where I am, I always wake up at 4:30 a.m. local time.'

'When I wasn't working out,' Lucas told me, 'I felt more tired during the day, and I found it harder to sleep at night. Now I work out a lot, and as a result, sleep is easy for me. A good workout does two things. First, the body is forced to recover, so it puts you into a sound sleep to achieve recovery. Second, the

---

[18] Exclusive discussion with John Jamar, March 2008.
[19] Exclusive discussion with Ray Titus, July 2008.
[20] Exclusive discussion with William Kirwan, May 2008.

endorphins reduce your stress, making it easier to get to sleep. I'm too cheap to buy drugs, so I exercise to generate them myself.'

After that quip, Lucas gave me another tip on getting to sleep. He told me: 'Before going to bed I'm careful not to do a heavy mental exercise that will keep me up for another hour.'[21]

The CEO of LifeLock doesn't have trouble sleeping either. Todd Davis told me: 'I usually crash hard after a good efficient day. I usually do not have trouble sleeping. I sleep soundly.'[22]

As for the CEO of Red Hat, Jim Whitehurst says he loves to sleep. 'You always hear about folks who sleep four hours a night. I know there are some people like that, but I can't live that way. I don't think very well if I'm sleep deprived. I have to be very disciplined to make sure I get the sleep I need. I get somewhere around seven hours' sleep a night. On the weekends I try to get eight.'

He told me: 'I generally go to bed comfortable with what I've done during the day and sleep well. Exercise helps, and I generally don't have caffeine after one or two o'clock in the afternoon. Some people think sleep is not a good use of your time. I disagree.'[23]

Some of the CEOs I just mentioned sleep less than the seven-and-a-half-hour average. Does this imply that you must have lower than average sleep needs to have better than average productivity? Not at all.

Consider this. Albert Einstein needed ten to eleven hours' sleep a night, which is far more than the average. Was he productive? Put it this way, while he had a full-time job at the patent office in Berne, Switzerland, in his spare time after work he wrote two of the most influential scientific papers ever.

Manuel Esquivel, who was prime minister of Belize, says: 'I sleep very well. When I go to bed I fall asleep within ten minutes. I've never had a problem sleeping, no matter what the circumstances.

---

[21] Exclusive discussion with Lucas Skoczkowski, April 2008.
[22] Exclusive discussion with Todd Davis, March 2008.
[23] Exclusive discussion with Jim Whitehurst, April 2008.

During a crisis it might take a little longer, but I still fall asleep and sleep well. In such a situation I make sure I think things through long before going to bed. Then when it's time for bed, there's no more work for my brain to do. It's sorted out and I can sleep.'[24]

Sleep debt and its effects

Some sleep experts say that, for every hour of shut eye you lose, you need to catch up at some point with a full hour of sleep. According to this school of thought, sleep debt accumulates hour for hour – so, for example, if for two weeks you get one hour less sleep per night than you normally need, you will need to pay back that debt by sleeping an extra 14 hours somewhere down the line. Other experts think that your catch-up sleep is more efficient, because when you're deprived, you quickly fall into a deep slumber and a larger percentage of your sleep is rapid eye movement (REM) sleep, which is what seems to be essential for restoration. Experts in this second group think that you don't need to pay back the debt exactly hour for hour.

TIP #19

Don't try to cut back on sleep. It will catch up on you – and when it does, you'll crash hard.

Regardless of which of the two schools of thought turns out to be right about how you pay it back, all researchers agree that sleep debt accumulates. You don't just get used to it. You have to pay it back somehow. Experts also agree that while you are sleep deprived your performance drops dramatically. Your intellectual ability, your mood, and your physical abilities all suffer. To illustrate this point, take the case of the Exxon Valdez accident. Many people remember it as having been caused by a drunken pilot. This turns out not to be true. When the case was studied more closely, investigators quickly came to the conclusion that the pilot was sleep deprived.

---

[24] Exclusive discussion with Manuel Esquivel, June 2008.

It's not surprising that a person lacking in shut eye was mistaken for somebody who was drunk. Studies have shown that sleep deprivation has similar effects to intoxication. The state of New Jersey has recognised this, and has even enacted laws punishing sleep-deprived drivers in the same way they punish drunk drivers.

If you're feeling drowsy during the day, it's because you're sleep deprived. The converse is not true: you might be sleep deprived, but not feel drowsy while you're doing something stimulating. As soon as you stop doing whatever it is that keeps you awake, you'll start to feel sleepy again.

For more about this subject, see Epstein (2007) and Dement and Vaughan (1999).

The amount of sleep you need

According to experts, most people need seven and a half hours a night, plus or minus around one hour. As is true with the distribution of any trait across a population, there is a good deal of variation. Each person has his or her own sleep requirements – the important thing is to recognise what yours are. As we discussed earlier, the more you deprive yourself of the sleep you need, the harder your brain tries to force you to get that sleep.

Lucas Skoczkowski, the 35-year-old CEO of Redknee, says he needs about six hours a night. 'Sure, there is some variation in how much sleep people need,' he said. 'So some people wind up with a little more waking time than others. That's just a fact of life. The worst thing you can do is fight against your own personal sleep needs. Don't try to reduce your sleep – this will certainly lower your performance.'

Lucas thinks that 'everybody knows how much sleep they need by the time they're young adults. You can't get away from that. If you cut back on sleep, you become much less productive – especially when work involves mental activity. It's the worst thing you can do. I have tried that, by the way. I wound up making a bunch of mistakes. You appear to be going faster, when actually you're slowing down.'[25]

---

[25] Exclusive discussion with Lucas Skoczkowski, April 2008.

Ray Kroc started and ran McDonald's. One of the most successful business people of all time, he made it a point to get a good night's sleep.

He wrote in his autobiography (Kroc with Anderson 1977) that people were always surprised at how fresh he was in the morning. He was always ready to go because he worked out a way of clearing his mind at night to sleep soundly.

Take Patrick Quinlan's advice. Besides being CEO of Ochsner Health Systems, Pat is also a medical doctor. He says: 'If you listen to your body, it will tell you the amount of sleep you need. That's one of the reasons regularity in your sleep is so important. You can construct your sleep cycles in a way that's reproducible. It's not just the duration; it's also the quality of the sleep that counts. There's no one size fits all when it comes to physiology. That's for sure. Everyone needs a different amount of sleep.'[26]

Solving sleep problems

Recognising the importance of sleep, some CEOs have worked out interesting ways of assuring they get enough of it. For example, Janice Chaffin, president of the consumer group in Symantec, keeps a notepad by her bed. 'If I'm thinking about too many things and have trouble sleeping,' she says, 'I write a note to myself. This lets me forget about it for the moment, because I know I'll get on it in the morning.'[27]

Ray Titus said: 'In 23 years of running this organisation I have never missed a night of sleep. I sleep from 12 midnight to six-thirty, typically. I get around six and a half hours' sleep a night. I can't go to bed too early.'

'Whatever it is you're thinking about at the end of the day,' advises Ray, 'take a piece of paper and a pen and write it down. Anything you're thinking about – anything at all – just write it down. Then go to sleep.'

---

[26] Exclusive discussion with Patrick Quinlan, April 2008.
[27] Exclusive discussion with Janice Chaffin, March 2008.

Ray recalls: 'In college people used to tell me how energetic I was. My battery was always running, so to speak. I just went so hard during the day – and just gave it all I had – so by the time bedtime came around I was exhausted. I think lazier people – or people who don't do as much throughout the day – have more trouble sleeping. I'm physically and mentally exhausted at the end of the day. I give everything I have to my work, I give everything I have to my family, and then I'm completely exhausted. It's an upward spiral. If I sleep well, I have a lot of energy during the day. If I have a lot of energy during the day I put out all I've got and am exhausted by the time I go to bed. Then I sleep really well, and so on and so forth.'[28]

Some people have trouble sleeping because they go to bed with too much on their minds. Another thing that keeps people awake at night is that their sleep cycle is thrown off. Experts agree that our bodies are subject to daily rhythms, and light is the most powerful cue keeping us in line. Exposure to light at the wrong time of day can upset your cycle and adversely affect your sleep/wake pattern. Sleep researchers hold that since the invention of the light-bulb, just over a hundred years ago, we have tended to throw off our rhythms by exposing ourselves to bright light at night. It's widely believed that because of this, on average each of us sleeps about an hour and a half less per night than our ancestors did before the invention of the light-bulb. So, as much as possible it's best to keep the lights dim before bedtime.

Keeping a regular schedule is also important. If you can stick to a regular sleep schedule throughout the week, you'll generally sleep better, and thereby maintain peak performance. Finally, experts advise us to avoid stimulating mental activities before going to bed. For example, try not to watch a scary movie or work on a complex problem. And it's best to avoid the temptation to check email just before going to bed. (Epstein 2007; Dement and Vaughan 1999)

---

[28] Exclusive discussion with Ray Titus, July 2008.

BALANCED LIFE

Juha Christensen is credited with having developed the idea for Symbian, the operating system company – he wrote the business plan and negotiated investments worth $130 million. He has started and run several other high-tech companies. Recognising his contributions, *Time* magazine named Juha one of the 25 most influential Europeans in technology.

His observation on working long hours is: those who work the longest hours are usually the least productive over time. There's value in hard work, but you need clear boundaries. Maintain hobbies and have a good family life.[29]

'You have to be physically and mentally present wherever you are,' says Daniel Doimo. 'If you are with your family, be with your family. If you are at work, be at work. Of course you might be tempted to deal with work issues while you are with your family, but you have to minimize that.'[30]

'I make sure to spend time with my family,' Todd Davis said. 'When your personal life is in order, I can assure you, you are more productive at work. I follow the adage of Ben Franklin: early to bed, early to rise. I go to bed most nights at about 10 o'clock and wake up most mornings at around four-thirty. That allows me to start my day right, and spend some time with the kids. I have twin boys who get up around five or five-thirty. I get about an hour with them before heading out to the gym, and from there out to the office.'[31]

Suri says: 'I spread my work out in such a way as to not compromise my family life. This is important. When things are going well in the family, you are free to concentrate on your work.'[32]

---

[29] Exclusive discussion with Juha Christensen, April 2008.
[30] Exclusive discussion with Daniel Doimo, March 2008.
[31] Exclusive discussion with Todd Davis, March 2008.
[32] Exclusive discussion with K. Surivakumar (Suri), March 2008.

Lucas Skoczkowski says this of his work day: 'I'm in the office by seven in the morning and get home by five-thirty in the afternoon. From five-thirty to eight at night, I spend all my time with my family.'[33]

Along these lines Janice Chaffin said: 'Most people need both family and work. Family is where you get intimacy, and work is where you make money and achieve self-actualization. Even people who do not need to work for money still need work to fill another account: self-actualization. Given that, you really need to pay attention to all the different parts of your life. Ignoring one will cause things to fall apart somewhere down the line.'[34]

Ray Titus said: 'I have had great days; I have had horrible days. I never take it home with me. I have a wife of 18 years. I will ask her opinion on things. We will talk about things. Other than that, I never bring my work home. I have a family. I'm committed to being a great husband and family man. That's top on my list.'[35]

Maintaining hobbies

The President of Tulane University, Scott Cowen, says: 'I take time every day for myself and my family. I also take vacation time. This is important for your own wellbeing; and it also has the side-effect of making you more effective. I enjoy reading and fishing. I'm most relaxed when I'm out on my boat during the summer out in the bay someplace with a fishing line over the board. I might not even be catching anything, but it's a mindless activity I simply enjoy.'[36]

Scott was emphasising how important it is to take time off to do other things. Play time is just as important as exercise, diet, and sleep. It makes you more effective when you go back to work. The paradox is that you can't do it with the intention of working better. True play is not done with an objective in mind – true play has no purpose. Besides, regardless of what play does for your productivity, is life really worth living without play?

---

[33] Exclusive discussion with Lucas Skoczkowski, April 2008.
[34] Exclusive discussion with Janice Chaffin, March 2008.
[35] Exclusive discussion with Ray Titus, July 2008.
[36] Exclusive discussion with Scott Cowen, March 2008.

Like Scott Cowen, Jim Holbrook likes to fish. 'I go fishing a couple of times a year,' Jim told me. 'That to me is great therapy. If you're thinking about work, you're not catching fish. If you focus on one thing – catching the fish – it pushes everything else to the back of your mind, and it all kind of sorts itself out. When I'm standing in the stream fishing I might think 10 minutes went by, but four hours passed. It's because I'm really present.'[37]

TIP #20

Don't forget to play. And when you play, do so with no purpose.

Everybody has his or her own hobby. For example, Randy Rose of Schwabe North America got his pilot's license last year.[38] Ray Titus coaches basketball at a high school, for which he gets a great sense of satisfaction – he feels 'the power of giving'.[39] But my favourite is Thierry Grange. While he's not running one of the top-ranked business schools in Europe, Thierry rides around the French Alps on his Ducati motorcycle.[40]

Taking time off

Some people understand the importance of taking time off. Frequently these are the most productive people. In his autobiography Lee Ioccoca (1984) says that during all of the time he was CEO of Ford Motors or of Chrysler he rarely worked weekends. And as an example of what a prime minister might do on weekends, Manuel Esquivel told me: 'A lot of times on the weekend I get out of town. I have a house by the sea – an hour's drive from here. It allows me to take my mind off work.'[41]

People who work too much become inefficient. Perhaps it's for this reason that Paul Kruse makes it a company requirement that people take time off. He told me: 'One of our policies at Blue Bell

---

[37] Exclusive discussion with Jim Holbrook, March 2008.
[38] Exclusive discussion with Randy Rose, March 2008.
[39] Exclusive discussion with Ray Titus, July 2008.
[40] Exclusive discussion with Thierry Grange, April 2008.
[41] Exclusive discussion with Manuel Esquivel, June 2008.

Creameries is that you have to take a full week off at some time during the year. You get in trouble if you don't.'

'Just like everybody else in the company, I take a full week,' Paul said. 'I use that time to go antelope hunting in west Texas. I take my cell phone with me. Every year, I don't get a phone call from the office. People go on doing their jobs and working things out on their own. They make it a point not to call me – I guess nobody wants to be the first to call.'

'I get so lonely during that week,' Paul lamented. 'I call the head assistant and ask her if everything is okay. It always is. It does feel lonely when not a single person needs me during that week. But in reality this means the organisation is working as it should. The terrible CEO is the one who is on the golf course and has to answer his or her cell phone on every hole to answer a question. There's a company that has problems.'[42]

Gilles du Chaffaut says it's good to keep a 'secret garden' – a place you go and people you see separate from your work and from your usual circle of friends. The city manager of Grenoble, France told me: 'It's good to have acquaintances different from the people you spend most of your time with. This allows you to get away and take on a different perspective. You'd be surprised how often you get new solutions to old problems by going off into your secret garden from time to time.'

'One of my hobbies is to hunt,' Gilles said. 'In France you have all sorts of people who hunt: people from the extreme upper class to good old country folk. I hunt with them all. It's very enriching because I spend time with people I don't often see. I learn all sorts of new things and I come back renewed.'[43]

BIORHYTHMS

'I learned you can't fight your natural biorhythms, because you're sure to lose the fight.' That's what Gary Stockman, CEO of Porter

---

[42] Exclusive discussion with Paul Kruse, March 2008.
[43] Exclusive discussion with Gilles du Chaffaut, November 2008.

Novelli, told me. 'Most people are either morning people or night people. I'm a morning person, so if there's something that requires a great deal of my concentration, it generally goes down better in the morning. Other things are better suited to my afternoon and evening temperament.'[44]

Serial entrepreneur Juha Christensen said: 'I try to figure out when I do my best thinking. That's different from person to person, but in my case, I happen to do my best thinking in the morning. So if I need to think a lot – for example, develop a strategy, have a brainstorming meeting – I tend to do that in the early hours. I have a bit of email time in the morning when I come in. That's a half hour, 45 minutes. Following that is a two-hour chunk of time I spend working on things that need my best thinking. Following that I might have a meeting or so. Then I have more email time.'

'No one is completely productive and a top performer eight, ten, or twelve hours a day,' he said. 'Some people are sprinters; others are marathon runners. Nobody runs ten or twelve hours a day. It's very important to be cognizant of that. First, don't beat yourself up about the fact that you might have some lows during the day. Second, use your understanding of your highs and lows to figure out what the best times are for you to do different kinds of things.'

Juha continued: 'Athletes have all these people around them telling them what works best, coaching them, and helping them find peak performance. But even the best figure skaters, for example, have times when they're down. They work intensively in interval training, but then they stop. It's the same for anything you do. I think it's very important to put that down time into your schedule as well.'

TIP #21

Accept that you will have down time. Don't beat yourself up over it. Enjoy it. And if it occurs around the same time every day, schedule it.

---

[44] Exclusive discussion with Gary Stockman, March 2008.

'For many people, this is just after lunch,' Juha believes. 'If this is the case for you, recognize it and plan to sit around and read magazines or socialize during that time. Allow yourself to have that down time. Don't get into a mode where you feel bad or stressed about it. Otherwise, you'll wind up feeling unfulfilled at the end of the day. It's perfectly natural to have down time.'

Juha summarised: 'It's important to understand when your peaks and down times are. Analyze it over a two-week period and revisit that analysis from time to time to make sure you have it roughly right. Once you understand your rhythms try to align your schedule accordingly.'[45]

Randy Rose, CEO of Schwabe North America and former Chief Operating Officer (COO) of Energizer Holdings, agrees. He says: 'I consider what my current energy level is and, based on that, assess when is an appropriate time to do a given task. If I need to do something creative I need to have a certain kind of energy; if I need to get into a conflictual situation, I need the energy for that. I might plan to do these things the following morning when I know I will have a good energy level. Throughout the day I ask myself what are the two or three things I can do now based on my current energy level.'[46]

> James D. White is President and CEO of Jamba Juice. Before that he was Senior Vice President for Safeway Stores.
>
> James thinks about biorhythms over extended periods – months and quarters. He likes to plan his efforts over long periods, pouring it on at critical points and working at a more relaxed pace during other times.[47]

'Make sure you schedule things according to your biorhythms,' Lucas Skoczkowski advises. 'For example, in the morning I do my serious reading and I do the things that require a lot of thinking.

---

[45] Exclusive discussion with Juha Christensen, April 2008.
[46] Exclusive discussion with Randy Rose, March 2008.
[47] Exclusive discussion with James White, April 2008.

In the afternoon I do more people-oriented tasks and talking. Evenings I spend most of my time with my son. Then I do some casual reading and spend time talking with my wife after my son goes to sleep. I pack an hour and a half of workout into my day as well. That creates a cadence. You might even call it a virtuous cycle, because the different activities feed each other.'[48]

You may not know ahead of time how you'll feel at certain times of the day. Sometimes it's best to leave yourself room to pick and choose what you do as your mood changes. For example, Gilles du Chaffaut told me he makes sure he has several different kinds of things to do during a given day. He can work on one or the other based on factors such as his temperament, energy level, or level of concentration.[49]

Discovering your biorhythms
To get an objective view of your daily rhythms you can use a simple technique. Once an hour rate yourself on a scale from one (very low) to five (very high) as to how you feel along these four different dimensions:

- **Physical energy:** your ability to do exercise;
- **Concentration:** your ability to focus on one thing;
- **Wakefulness:** how awake you feel;
- **Outlook:** how optimistic you feel.

It may not be practical to take notes every hour. If that's the case, you can do some of the hours one day and other hours another day, until you get a full day's view. You should do this several times so as to get an average.

Finding what drives you
Not only is it important to understand when you have the appropriate energy and temperament for a given task; it's also important to understand what motivates you. What will give you the most mental energy?

---

[48] Exclusive discussion with Lucas Skoczkowski, April 2008.
[49] Exclusive discussion with Gilles du Chaffaut, November 2008.

On this subject Jim Whitehurst told me: 'I don't think of myself as personally disciplined in every aspect of my life, but if I have some passion behind what I'm doing, that drives discipline. I look to do things that have some social benefit; things I really care about deep inside. Otherwise, it's hard to be motivated. Unless you have an incredible capacity for self-control, you won't be able to do something you don't like doing for very long. Some people have that much self-control, but the vast majority of us don't. You can't just work like an efficient machine. Human beings need passion to drive them.'

Jim said: 'For example, at Red Hat I feel that we are doing a social good by offering Open Source software. I feel good about what I'm doing and feel that my efforts will make a difference.'[50]

TIP #22

You aren't a machine. You need passion to drive you. Conversely, if you hate what you're doing, it will drag you down in the long run.

Perhaps we can close this chapter with some thoughts from Richard Branson (2004) on where he gets his energy. He says that what drives him most is to be able to use his creative ability. If he can't have fun and be creative in business, he isn't interested. He advises that if making money is your only motive, you're probably better off not doing it. Branson says that in business and in extreme sports a lot of his energy comes from the thrill of achieving what first appears unachievable. In facing challenges with a team, he thrives on the camaraderie that inevitably develops among team members.

These are the things that keep Richard Branson energised.

---

[50] Exclusive discussion with Jim Whitehurst, April 2008.

HABITS

For one week work on these two habits.

Habit 3: Maintain a lifestyle that will give you maximum energy
This means doing aerobic exercise at least three times a week for an hour each session, eating a light lunch, and getting enough sleep. For some people this is a tall order, but remember that Master The Moment consists of steps to work on and progress in an ongoing manner. If you're starting from zero, develop this habit slowly.

Habit 4: Listen to your biorhythms and organise your day accordingly
Make it a habit to always listen to your biorhythms and, based on what you learn, to make adjustments to how you plan to spend your time. If you're more creative in the morning, schedule creative activities for the morning; if you're more sociable in the afternoon, schedule relationship-building activities for the afternoon.

How to work on habits
Here's a reminder of the procedure. In the morning think about the day's events that will allow you to reinforce these two habits. During the day take every opportunity to make them automatic. As a visual reminder, put this book, or a copy of this page, somewhere you can see it from time to time throughout the day. In the evening take five minutes to rate yourself on a scale of 1 to 5, with 1 indicating that you did very badly on the habit and 5 indicating that you did very well. Pencil in a rating for that day on the chart below.

HABIT	DAYS						
	1	2	3	4	5	6	7
Maintain lifestyle for energy.							
Listen to your biorhythms.							

EXERCISES

Here are some exercises you can do over the next week or so to help work the ideas from this chapter into your own life.

i   If you aren't getting aerobic exercise three days a week for at least 20 minutes a day, make time for it over the next week. Keep it light at first, so that you don't wear yourself out. See if it makes you feel more energetic. Gradually work exercise into a weekly routine.

ii Over the next week, make a note of what you eat for lunch and also note how your energy level fluctuates throughout the day. If what you eat is bringing you down, try changing your eating habits for a week and notice the difference. Gradually change your eating habits on a permanent basis.

iii If you aren't getting enough sleep, make fixing the problem a priority. That will be a good use of your time.

iv Start thinking about how you feel at different times of the day. When is your down time? When is it best for you to perform intellectual activity? If you have to be firm with somebody, what time of day is generally best for you to do that?

v   Go back to the list you made in Exercise (iii) from the first chapter. Over the next few weeks make a conscious effort to find a healthy and sustainable balance in the time you put into the different roles you play.

6 PRIORITISE

You've probably gathered in reading up to this point that the high achievers featured in this book aren't necessarily doing more than anybody else. What really sets them apart is the choices they make to do the things with the highest impact. They select worthy goals and focus on them through completion.

As Lucas Skoczkowski said, 'Managing time is simple. That is, if you can get prioritization right. This is something that's challenging for everybody. When asked, everybody will say they prioritize. Very few people really do it. If you prioritize to the point where you no longer have time, you aren't prioritizing enough.'

He went on to tell me how his attitude on prioritisation has changed over time. 'In the last five years it really dawned on me that of my 10 or so priorities there were really one or two items that matter far more than the others,' he said. 'All the other things appeared urgent or flashy, but those one or two things were what really needed doing.'

> CEO of Redknee, a communications software company providing products for wireless networks, Lucas Skoczkowski is on a fast track. He was recently honoured with the Top 40 Under 40 Award for Canada.
>
> He says you have to be ruthless about priorities. Pick one or two things that really need to get done.

'I believe all of us go through at least three stages in life,' Lucas said. 'During the first stage we think the faster we do things and the more things we do, the more value that creates. Then we learn and figure out we need to prioritize, but we continue to try to do a lot of things. During the third and final stage we refine the idea from the second stage, and we learn to pick out the one or two things that really have to get done – the one or two things that hold 80 per cent of the value. We make sure those one or two things get done. To move from phase two to phase three you have to learn that to go faster you need to slow down.'

Lucas reckons he is probably moving from the second stage to the third stage. 'Hopefully, by the time I'm 40 I'll be squarely in the third stage. It really comes down to understanding what it is you are trying to achieve and why, and understanding how important it is in terms of your other priorities. You need to be ruthless on priorities.'[1]

---

[1] Exclusive discussion with Lucas Skoczkowski, April 2008.

Gary Stockman runs Porter Novelli, a global marketing services firm headquartered in New York City. Gary's also an avid cyclist.

His advice: make sure you take care of the big things. The little things will fall into place.[2]

To prioritise, you have to be able to recognise what's most important. Then you have to focus on those things, setting the less important aside until you have bits of free time to work on them. To do this you have to be good at judging what's most important. You'll never have perfect information, so you have to get good at determining when you know enough to make a decision. Once you set your priorities, you have to maintain your focus. This means turning down opportunities and politely refusing all requests that don't fit into your priorities.

A key principle of time management is not to try to do it all.

CHOOSING WHAT TO DO

Given that you can't do it all, the best thing you can do is select the right things to do. Paul Orfalea was acutely aware of this as he was building Kinko's into the huge success it became. He writes in his autobiography (Orfalea and Marsh 2007) that he was once told that most people never do the big things in life. Determined not to let that happen in his life, he would maintain a list of big things and would keep an eye on that list to make sure he got those things done.

TIP #23

It's far more effective to do the right things than it is to do things right.

Similarly, Todd Davis, CEO of LifeLock, says there's no way you could do everything that's available for you to do. There are just

[2] Exclusive discussion with Gary Stockman, March 2008.

too many things coming your way. 'I try to understand my priorities and mission in my role,' he told me. 'When presented with a list of what's available for me to do, I choose those things that are in line with my priorities and mission and cut off those that aren't. I either delegate those activities not in line with my mission or I respectfully decline.'[3]

Nick Mueller says: 'I'm probably not the most efficient person, but I make up for it by learning a great deal of what I need to know to make good decisions. You have to know what the right things to do are. Very careful planning about your larger goals and clear vision of where you're going is most important. I don't think I'm very good at time management in the sense of making the best use of every hour. But I think I have a strong focus on priorities.'[4]

In the same vein, Paul Kruse of Blue Bell Creameries told me with a straight face: 'I don't know if I'm any good at time management, but I tend to get done what I want to get done.'[5]

Your direction

This reminds me of a high school teacher I know who says she feels she is able to get done the things she considers important, and she never feels overwhelmed. This is not to say that she doesn't have a full load. On any given day she might have classes to prepare, papers to grade, and four or five hours of actual teaching time. She also has two children of her own in primary school, and she has a husband who works long hours, leaving it to her to do most of the cooking.

The reason she feels relaxed about what she does is that she has a strong sense of who she is and what she wants in life. Family is important to her, and teaching satisfies her need to help children develop. She doesn't have to think too hard about what her priorities are, because out of her clear mission falls a set of activities she considers important.

---

[3] Exclusive discussion with Todd Davis, March 2008.
[4] Exclusive discussion with Gordon Mueller, April 2009.
[5] Exclusive discussion with Paul Kruse, March 2008.

The CEO of Ochsner Health Systems feels the same way. 'When we talk about priorities, what we're talking about is a sense of purpose,' Patrick Quinlan believes. 'As I said before, I think it's important to inspect your life. Often when you have a group of priorities without an overarching purpose, you have an illusion of organization, when in fact you're just organizing junk.'

He expanded on this. 'Once you have a strategy then you can start to segregate what you do. It's not just about what you do in a given week, it's about your life plan. You can only have a rough plan; if it's too specific, it just can't work. There are too many variables in the future, and you can't anticipate them. At least when you have a general strategy in your life, you have a general framework into which you can work all the components. Then as you get down to thinking of what you want to do in a week, a month, a season, a year, a decade, or even a lifetime, you have a system of values against which you can test your options.'[6]

The lesson here is to understand first what your mission is. Based on that, keep a list of long-term goals. Most people have different roles in life, so you can expect to have different missions, and hence different lists of priorities. Update your lists as things change. Remember that a list of goals is not a Holy Grail; it's just a tool to help you maintain focus.

When determining what's important, James White of Jamba Juice advises: 'Go for high impact. Find the highest leverage priorities to deliver the overall objectives.'[7]

Steve Simpson, former CEO of Extended Systems, adds: 'Pick what you have an edge in and gravitate towards that. Eliminate the losing activities as quickly as you can.'[8]

Different kinds of priorities

When setting priorities it's important to note that all tasks should not be treated in the same way. For example, things like networking don't fit into time slots in the same way as

---

[6] Exclusive discussion with Patrick Quinlan, April 2008.
[7] Exclusive discussion with James White, April 2008.
[8] Exclusive discussion with Steve Simpson, March 2008.

administrative tasks or tasks with tangible output do. When building relationships with people you have to be more flexible with your time. It would be most distracting to others if you were watching the clock as you were talking with them.

As James Ravannack, cofounder of Superior Energy Services, puts it, 'How do you prioritize doing things with your children? How do you prioritize working with your best customer? You can't do it. You have to take these kinds of things as they come.'[9]

If, on the other hand, you're dealing with people and you need to get to the point quickly, you might set up an environment that fosters more direct conversation. For example, if you have a standing table in your office, and you hold meetings around that table, you'll find meeting attendees never get comfortable – and, consequently, that they get to the point more quickly.

Many of the CEOs advise being a little parsimonious with your time in meetings and formal activities. But be generous with your time where you're communicating to groups of people who deal with your customers, or when you're communicating to customers themselves. You also want to spend the time and invest the resources in developing a clear idea of what you want to do and how you want to do it – how you want to improve on what you did last year.

Steve Hansel, former CEO of Hibernia National Bank, said: 'I tried to leave time for walking around and visiting with employees where they were. I tried to leave a lot of time for communicating with employees and customers. Those were all priorities. I've always had an open-door policy. Anybody, from tellers to my direct reports, could walk in. If I wasn't busy at that moment I'd talk with them.'[10]

Making the difference between people time and task time is an ongoing learning experience. Randy Rose of Schwabe North America relates: 'I used to be so focused on my objectives that somebody knocking on the door to tell me something would be a terrible distraction to me. I have since learned that what that person brings

---

[9] Exclusive discussion with James Ravannack, April 2009.
[10] Exclusive discussion with Steve Hansel, March 2008.

forward may be critical to our total business. What I used to consider a distraction I now consider a potential opportunity to accelerate progress. Now when I'm interrupted I try to change my focus and pay attention to the person who has come to see me.'

TIP #24

Time spent dealing with people should not be prioritised in the same way as time spent doing a task alone. When you're dealing with people, it would be detrimental to the relationship if you tried to rush through the interaction.

Randy even refines the notion of people time, by making sure he spends enough time with each group of people. 'I associate priorities with the different kinds of relationships I have,' he told me. 'I have a set of priorities for employee relationships, a set for lenders, a set for customers, a set for personal relationships, and so on.'[11]

Brit Kirwan told me something similar. 'As chancellor of the University of Maryland, my responsibility covers 13 different institutions. When I look at who are my constituents, it is an unbelievably broad array of individuals and groups: students, faculty, staff, alumni, business owners, the government, the general public, and the K through 12 schools[12] – the K through 12 schools are where we get our students. The interests of the different constituents are often not aligned. In fact, they have competing interests. For example, the students don't want you to raise tuition, but the faculty wants you to, because without it they can't get a raise. My challenge is to be sure I spend the appropriate amount of time with the various constituents. If you just allow events to take their natural course, you could just wind up not spending time with some constituents – not intentionally, but just through the course of events. My staff and I work hard to ensure I allocate my time appropriately to the various constituents – so nobody gets left out.'[13]

---

[11] Exclusive discussion with Randy Rose, March 2008.
[12] Schools in the USA that teach pupils below the age of 18.
[13] Exclusive discussion with William Kirwan, May 2008.

How computers prioritise

So far we've been talking about how human beings prioritise. But there's also something to learn on this subject from our silicon-based friends. How do computers give the appearance of doing so many different things at once? How do they set priorities to ensure that all things get done eventually, and that the most important things get done first? Let's take a closer look.

For our purposes, we can compare a single-CPU computer with a single person, and the different tasks the computer has the opportunity to perform with the different tasks that are before the person at a given time. Just like a person, a computer has several different types of tasks: human interface tasks (for example, interacting with a user who is editing a document), important non-interactive tasks (for example, running a payroll program in the background), and administrative tasks (such as swapping programs in and out of memory). This is similar to the kinds of tasks you might have before you. User-interactive tasks are like those where you collaborate with people. Important non-interactive tasks are like those you need to carry out uninterrupted. And the computer's administrative tasks are like the various administrative tasks you can't avoid doing.

A computer operating system makes a scheduling decision at four different times:

- **When a new task is created by the current one:** In this case, the decision is whether to start executing the new task (to the possible detriment of the current one), or to queue the new task for execution later. This is similar to the situation where you're working on something uninterrupted, but in the process you come up with something new that has to get done. You immediately have to decide whether to set aside what you're doing to focus on the new task or to jot down enough information about the new task so that you can go back to it later.

- **When a task is finished:** At this point the operating system goes back to deciding what task to perform next. This is similar to the way you might work through your top five list during the day. Once you've finished one thing, you have to decide what to do next.

- **When the current task reaches a point where it's waiting for something to happen:** For example, the task may be waiting for a disk read and has no use for the CPU in the meantime. The operating system then decides what other task it might put the CPU to work on. This is like the times when you're waiting for somebody to call you back before you can move forward with something. There's nothing you can do to move the project forward until that person calls, so you might as well do something else in the meantime.

- **When an interruption occurs:** The interruption could be the completion of a disk read, for example indicating that the event another process was waiting for has now occurred. This is like getting the call you were waiting for to enable you to carry on with your work. An interruption might also occur when a timer goes off, indicating that the time allotted to perform a task has expired. This is similar to what you do when you set aside two hours to work on something without interruption. When the two hours are up, you need to make a decision on what to do next.

A variety of strategies are used for assigning the computer's attention to the different tasks in a way that allows each one to progress, and at the same time to give users the impression that they are the most important thing in the world. Which strategy is employed is based on a set of tradeoffs that depend on the policy of the system. For example, the policy might be to maximise the number of jobs completed per hour, to maximise response time, or to be as predictable as possible. Again it's easy to see how similar this is to the way people juggle priorities.

Some of the different strategies used by operating systems are listed below. Of course there are different variations on each of these, but I summarise the points that are relevant to our discussion on time management for people. The main approaches are:

- **First come first served**, an algorithm in which the processor executes one task at a time in the order they come up;

- **Shortest remaining time first**, which has the processor execute whichever job it can finish in the least time;

121

- **Round-robin scheduling**, where the processor spends a fixed amount of time on one task and then goes on to the next, working through the queue and giving each task the same amount of time;

- **Priority scheduling**, where the operating system assigns a priority to each task. In the case where more than one task is assigned the same priority, the operating system decides between the tasks in a round-robin fashion. The CPU is given the highest-priority tasks first, and might even spend more time on high-priority tasks. The challenge here is to avoid working on the highest-priority task to the exclusion of all others. For example, the operating system certainly doesn't want to ignore the user while working on a high-priority background task.

As you can see, computers are up against the same problems as people. It's useful to review the strategies operating system designers use to try to get done as much as possible. Are there ways you can use these same ideas to get more out of your day?

Urgent versus important

When choosing what to do, you should make the difference between what's urgent and what's important. Some things are both urgent and important. These should be top priority. Other things are neither urgent nor important. These should be done only when you have nothing else to do.

A useful technique for setting priorities is to write them into a matrix of urgent versus important. This technique, attributed to Dwight D. Eisenhower, consists of evaluating tasks along two dimensions – their urgency and their importance. According to Eisenhower, 'What is important is seldom urgent, and what is urgent is seldom important.'

Managers using this technique should get personally involved in anything that's important. If it's also urgent, they should work on it immediately. If it's not urgent they should schedule it. As for anything that's not important, if it's urgent they should delegate the task. If it's not urgent, they should drop it.

This technique is also useful for people who are not managers, and it can be used in personal life as well as in work life. A home-maker who attended one of my seminars agreed to let me include her matrix in this book (Table 6.1) to illustrate the point further.

Table 6.1 Example list of tasks

	Urgent	Non-Urgent
Important	Get groceries for the week. Take kids to school. Pick up kids from school. Make dinner for tonight. Have lunch with friends.	Vacuum the house. Clean the kitchen. Water the plants. Work out with aerobics video.
Unimportant	Listen to telemarketer pitch. Watch news at noon.	Read ads that come in the mail.

The urgent tasks are those that have to be completed today. For those that are also important, she makes sure she schedules working on them at appropriate times during the day. For those that aren't important, she may or may not work on them, depending on whether they prevent her from doing what's important. For example, if telemarketers call while she's doing something important, she'll quickly dismiss them. Otherwise, she might listen to what they have to say. She likes to watch the news at noon, but it's less important than having lunch with friends, so she'll skip the news and spend time with her friends.

Lucas Skoczkowski told me: 'When confronted with an opportunity to do something, the first question I ask myself is, "Is this something that needs to be done?" Then I ask, "Is this something I need to do, or can I have somebody else do it?" I go through this thought process at work and at home. For example, at home when something needs fixing, I decide if I should spend my time doing it, or if I should hire somebody to do it.'

'Right off the bat, many things can be eliminated altogether,' he said. 'Either they are not worth doing at all, or somebody else can do it. If I do decide it's something for me to do myself, I then assign one of three priorities to it: Critical, Major, or Minor.'[14]

Thierry Grange offered his thoughts on setting priorities. 'The first thing to do when considering whether to do something is to see if it fits into the categories of things you do. In my case, I have four categories. I am an enabler to help people get things done. I work with people outside the school to promote the school. I make sure systems and processes in the school work. And finally I stimulate creativity and seek ideas. If a task that doesn't fit one of those categories comes my way, I immediately give it to somebody else.'

The president of one of the top business schools in Europe went on to say: 'Among the tasks I take on, I then prioritize. I base priorities on the impact it will have. For urgent tasks, I consider the value of doing it versus the consequences of not doing it. For non-urgent tasks, I look at the value of the outcome. I then make sure I allocate the right amount of time to the high-priority tasks.'[15]

TIP #25

What's important for you may not be the same as what's important to other people. Be careful to set your priorities based on what you want to accomplish – not based on what somebody else wants to accomplish.

Frank Stewart, the man who built Stewart Enterprises into a worldwide business in the death care industry, told me: 'You have to prioritize what's important to you. The choices you make are highly individual – what might be a big thing to you may not be big to me. Judgement is the important word here. You have to use your own good judgement as to what's big for you. And it's all relative. When something is "big," it's only big in comparison to something else.'

---

[14] Exclusive discussion with Lucas Skoczkowski, April 2008.
[15] Exclusive discussion with Thierry Grange, April 2008.

'I believe in writing down all my plans and intentions, and I keep a schedule,' Frank said. 'As I go through every day, I work through the things I have listed as important to me. If you don't plan, you're prone to losing sight of what you're trying to accomplish. You fall victim to all the various distractions that come your way throughout the day.'

He summarised his thoughts. 'Prioritizing means rating the various tasks you have an opportunity to carry out. You need good judgement to make good choices about what's important. Nothing's perfect. You just have to give it your best.'[16]

Making good choices about what's most important is indeed a worthy use of your time. Once you know what you want to do, you need to plan it.

PLANNING TO DO IT

Remember that you are usually planning without perfect information. Leave room to play things by ear. When you do your planning, remember your constraints. For example, you have to consider your boss's schedule or the schedule of anybody else you involve. Organise your work accordingly.

As James Carter points out, most plans aren't valid for long. Having spent 25 years as president of Loyola University in New Orleans, he challenges any executive to pull out a five-year plan from five years ago and show that things turned out as planned. 'Many things change,' he says. 'But you still need to have a plan. If you don't have a plan, you have no direction at all.'[17]

In Juha Christensen's opinion, 'The cardinal time management rule is the day needs to be scheduled ahead of time – preferably a few days beforehand, or even a week. I don't like to see any free time on my calendar. That doesn't mean I'm in meetings all the time. It could mean time working alone on a project – I schedule that too. Even goofing off I like to have scheduled, so I know my boundaries. I play tennis a couple of times a week. Every now and then I swim. These things are also scheduled.'

---

[16] Exclusive discussion with Frank Stewart, April 2008.
[17] Exclusive discussion with James Carter, April 2008.

'Of course, nothing is perfect,' Juha points out. 'I have days when my planning doesn't work as well as I expected. Things take longer than expected, or I receive a call at a time when I'm scheduled to do my best work.'

Daniel Doimo is president of a large part of APC by Schneider Electric, a $3.5 billion global organisation making uninterruptible power supplies (UPS). When the main power fails, his products make sure essential equipment stays running.

Daniel allocates 20 per cent of his time for dealing with emergencies. You know the unexpected is going to occur. Why not leave time in your plans to deal with whatever comes up? When you have that buffer time, emergencies are less likely to destroy your schedule.[18]

He continues: 'Successful days for me have very clear boundaries. I put the commute to and from work in my calendar – it's usually 15 minutes. I typically try to make sure I have conference calls during the drive time. Since my drive time is always of the same duration, it's easy for my assistant to fill that time with calls. In the morning I'm able to speak to people in Europe, and driving home in the evening I'm able to speak to people in Asia. That works out nicely.'

Juha went on to say: 'To-do lists are important. Keep fairly good track of to-do lists. Everybody has their own system. No system really works completely. You will always have more items on the list than you can get done. You have to make sure you put things on the list that are important, more so than urgent things. When you do your planning for the week, make sure you plan your meetings and tasks in accordance with your to-do list.'

Juha finished his thoughts on planning. 'A good three hours – maybe four hours – of my schedule every day is what I simply call dead time. That's when I do things like sign papers that come in or when I go through my to-do list and work on smaller items.'[19]

---

[18] Exclusive discussion with Daniel Doimo, March 2008.
[19] Exclusive discussion with Juha Christensen, April 2008.

Daniel Doimo projects his work activities over different time frames. 'I try to prioritize my tasks on a monthly, weekly, and daily basis,' he told me. 'I make sure it's all reasonable – that the daily and weekly tasks build up to complete the monthly tasks. Of course things don't always work out according to plan. We tend to overestimate what we can do in a day, and underestimate what we can do in a year. But because I have this planning discipline I'm able to take a long-term view and detect very early if I'll have any trouble meeting my objectives.'[20]

When I first talked with Ray Titus about time management, he told me: 'The first thing I can say about time management is what my father advised me. He was the founder and CEO of Minuteman Press. My father advised me to get some quiet time, for example on Sunday evening. Set aside an hour for yourself to think through your upcoming week. It's almost a mini strategic plan for the week. Of course you have things beyond your control that might already be scheduled, and other things will pop up during the week. If you set aside the quiet time to think things through it allows you to get on the offensive.'

'Some people are always on the defensive,' Ray said. 'They're always having to put their finger in the proverbial dyke to stop the flood. They spend their time putting out fires. These people never manage to get on the offensive. Part of the problem is they don't have their list of things they want to get done during the week. They just get through the week and do whatever comes their way.'

TIP #26

By planning you go on the offensive. You exercise more control over what gets done and when.

Ray is careful to avoid that mistake by trying hard to stay on the offensive. 'I go in with an offensive plan every week,' he told me. 'This means starting out with a huge list of things I want to get accomplished; then going through and putting initials next to items

---

[20] Exclusive discussion with Daniel Doimo, March 2008.

on the list. The initials indicate who I want to delegate a particular item to. Of course, being the CEO, I can delegate. For your readers who are not managers, a similar process would have them putting initials of people they want to ask for help on an item, or people they want to influence on a given subject. No matter what you're doing, you need to get other people involved. So these ideas apply to anybody – not just managers.'

Ray summarised this idea by telling me: 'This is time management 1-0-1. Sit down with a pen and paper on Sunday night and jot down what you want to get done during the week and who you want to involve. I'm a strong believer in the basics. You don't need a fancy computer to do this and it's a very simple idea. But it's also very powerful.'[21]

Ray Titus is not the only CEO who gets quiet time on Sunday evenings to plan what he'll do the next week. When he was CEO of Ford Motors and Chrysler, Lee Ioccoca planned his weeks every Sunday. He generally didn't work weekends, but he did set aside some time Sunday evening to plan the upcoming week. (Iacocca with Novak 1984)

A by-product of planning is that you get better at it as you go along. The more you get used to planning, the more you learn what you can really do – and the better you get at predicting how much time things take.

Long-term planning
James White has some good ideas on planning. The CEO of Jamba Juice says that when he plans he starts out with a long-term objective – for example, an annual result – and then he breaks that down into component objectives by quarter. 'From the quarterly objectives,' he says, 'you can then break it down further into subcomponent objectives almost on a weekly level. Ultimately, this should get you to the desired annual results.'[22]

Randy Rose of Schwabe North America says: 'I try to plan at least once a month. I adjust timelines, and revisit priorities and

---

[21] Exclusive discussion with Ray Titus, July 2008.
[22] Exclusive discussion with James White, April 2008.

overall objectives. Based on that thought process, I might make some decisions on what to change in how we deal with some aspect of our business. For example, we might make changes in how we deal with suppliers or in what critical things we do to develop our people.'[23]

I asked Jim Holbrook about planning. He said: 'I'm a believer in disciplined planning. We use the Objectives, Goals, Strategy, and Measures (OGSM) tool. You need to set objectives based on overall goals. You need a strategy to get where you're going, and you need milestones consisting of measurable results so you know you're making progress. Planning is important; the plan itself is not. It's the process more than the outcome that's important.'[24]

Brit Kirwan, Chancellor of the University System of Maryland, said: 'At the beginning of the year, I sit down with the people that report to me and after some discussion I identify my major goals for the year. What is it I want to achieve? And what do I need them to help me achieve? This comes to a short list – maybe a half dozen things. Then we audit the calendar throughout the year, to ensure I'm spending adequate time on each of the major goals so something isn't slipping through the cracks – and so at the end of the year we don't find I haven't paid enough attention to something.'[25]

And finally, Steve Hansel shared his ideas on planning. 'I always tried to plan my own time in a way where I did not get trapped into doing stuff I considered low priority. You have to be careful about over-planning. A wise man once told me that you'll agree to anything as long as it's long enough in advance. But the day of reckoning will come and you'll be telling yourself, "Geez – did I really agree to that?"'[26]

Daily top five list
'I want to be in control of the ball,' says Suri of American Reprographics. 'I don't want to be behind the ball chasing after it and being driven by it. I want to drive the ball. It's very important for me to come to my desk in the morning and decide what it is I have

---

[23] Exclusive discussion with Randy Rose, March 2008.
[24] Exclusive discussion with Jim Holbrook, March 2008.
[25] Exclusive discussion with William Kirwan, May 2008.
[26] Exclusive discussion with Steve Hansel, March 2008.

to do today. I don't want to come in and react. I want to be driving my job.'[27]

A very simple, but effective, tool to help you stay focused every day is a daily to-do list. You should keep the list to around five items. Why five? In 1956 cognitive psychologist George A. Miller wrote about this in a classic article called 'The Magical Number Seven, Plus or Minus Two'. Miller (1956) observed that the memory span for young adults is about seven 'chunks', where the term 'chunk' refers to the largest meaningful unit that the person recognises. For example, the idea that 'it's really important to keep daily top five lists' is a chunk for me. I don't have to look at the individual words in the sentence and consider them on their own. I might not even write that sentence out the same way each time. The idea itself is the meaningful unit.

And don't think you need to have as many as five. Some of the most effective people like to keep the list well below five. Take, for example, Jean-René Bouvier. Before starting Buzzinbees, he was vice president at HP in charge of a line of software products providing the signalling backbone for telephone networks. It's not rocket science, but it's very close to it.

Jean-René is clearly no slouch intellectually, but listen to what he says about the number of things he can keep track of. 'When considering the seven plus or minus two principle, I like the minus two part best. Five is already a lot to consider. In fact, three is the maximum number of priorities I can consider at a time.'[28]

The point of the top five list is not to finish everything in a given day. And not everything on the list has to be top priority. Some things can simply be reminders.

Mark Radtke likes this idea so much, he told me, that 'hands down the most effective time management tool for me is my top five list.' The CEO of Integrys Energy Services said: 'At the end of the day, or at the beginning of the next day, I identify the five most important things to work on. It's not at all uncommon to finish the day

---

[27] Exclusive discussion with K. Surivakumar (Suri), March 2008.
[28] Exclusive discussion with Jean-René Bouvier, April 2010.

without having taken care of all five tasks. The important thing is: it keeps me focused.'[29]

What do you put on your top five list? It should be a mix of things from different roles you play in life. It might include 'go get groceries' or 'buy a mother's day present'. And it might include 'work on presentation for shareholder meeting'. You can list things that have clear finishing points (for example, 'fill out tax forms'), and you can list things that are ongoing in nature (for example, 'walk around and talk to people to get their opinions').

As an example, here is my own top five list for today (see Figure 6.1). The items are in no particular order. I include a personal task ('buy new DVD player') and a workout ('ride bike up mountain'). I include two items I intend to finish ('finish partner brochure and send out to potential partners' and 'record radio programme') and one item I know I won't finish today ('work on "prioritise" chapter').

Figure 6.1 Example top five list

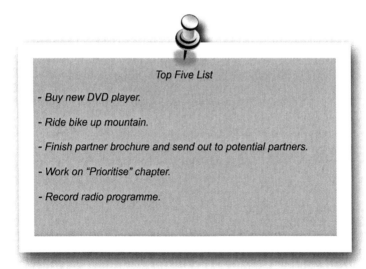

---

[29] Exclusive discussion with Mark Radtke, April 2008.

Leaving time for the unexpected

Daniel Doimo plans time for unexpected events. He estimates that 20 per cent of his time is taken by emergencies, so he works that time into his schedule. 'I always reserve time for crisis,' he says. 'These are things that are very important and very urgent. But I try to spend a lot of time on planning, and moving things forward. I actually put time in my calendar for emergencies. I allow about 20 per cent of my time for this.'[30]

Todd Davis does the same thing. 'I'm also very careful about how much time I allocate for unknowns,' he says. 'So I usually block out time – and it tends to be later in the day – to meet with other people to seek out what might need my attention.'[31]

Sometimes unexpected events turn out to be valuable opportunities. Nick Mueller calls these 'pop-ups'. He said: 'Some people chafe at this, but you have to take a look at them. Some of the most productive and meaningful decisions I've made weren't on the radar screen at the beginning of the year.'

TIP #27

Don't make your plans so rigid that unexpected events throw you off completely. Leave time in your schedule to react to events, and leave time just to think.

'You have to seize those opportunities when they come by,' Nick advised. 'People who operate in their comfort zone, wanting everything to be organized and planned, don't want to have to deal with something coming in out of left field. These people tend to get frustrated when these pop-ups arise. You have to be able to adjust to change.'[32]

Allowing for think time

Let's never forget the importance of choosing the right things to do. You can't do everything, so choosing where to apply your effort is

---

[30] Exclusive discussion with Daniel Doimo, March 2008.
[31] Exclusive discussion with Todd Davis, March 2008.
[32] Exclusive discussion with Gordon Mueller, April 2009.

one of your most important activities. You need to take the time to think and rethink your direction. For this reason, setting aside time just for reflection is itself one of the right things to do. Not surprisingly, most of the CEOs featured in this book are very much aware of when and where they do their best thinking.

For example, Steve Hansel says he likes to leave time for thinking while at work. 'I've always avoided being over-scheduled specifically for that reason,' he says.[33] In contrast, Randy Rose leaves time to go off to a quiet place to think. 'Sometimes I get away from the office and go to the public library to sit in a quiet place,' he told me. 'The change in environment helps me think.'[34]

Father Carter of Loyola University thinks best when he exercises. He said: 'Exercise allows you to subconsciously work on some of your big problems. In my case, the daily walking is my think time.'[35] And strange as it sounds, John Koerner says he has his best ideas just as he's waking up, in the nether land between waking and sleeping.[36]

Jim Holbrook does some of his best thinking while flying. 'I block off time for myself,' he says. 'Airplane travel provides me time to think. I keep a journal of cool stuff, good ideas. On the airplane I go back over these ideas and look for themes. When I am in the plane I'm shuffling papers and my seat area looks like a pig pen. The poor person sitting next to me must go crazy. But that's my time, and I really go at it.'[37]

Bill Gates goes off on his own for a week at a time to think. He calls these his 'think weeks' (Guth 2005).

You need to get away from daily business and clear your mind. Take the time to think about where you're going.

---

[33] Exclusive discussion with Steve Hansel, March 2008.
[34] Exclusive discussion with Randy Rose, March 2008.
[35] Exclusive discussion with James Carter, April 2008.
[36] Exclusive discussion with John Koerner, June 2008.
[37] Exclusive discussion with Jim Holbrook, March 2008.

Many chief executives go so far as to formally schedule think time. Bill Gates, certainly one of the most effective CEOs of our time, does exactly this. For over 12 years, Gates has been taking a week off twice a year to go away by himself to think. He calls these 'Think Weeks'. He used to take a stack of papers, read through them, and mark them up with his comments. Now he does all that electronically, reading papers on a computer and marking them up digitally. Gates also does a lot of his strategic thinking during this time. (Guth 2005)

Paul Orfalea says that when he was running Kinko's he would take several weeks off a year to go and do something else. He says this never hurt the bottom line – and, very much to the contrary, some of his best ideas came to him when he was away from work doing something else. 'When your mind can break free of all that worry and clutter, you will find yourself coming up with the most improbable and inspired ideas.' (Orfalea and Marsh 2007)

STICKING TO YOUR PRIORITIES

Thierry Grange told me: 'One of the important elements of good time management is your capacity to stay focused on objectives and priorities. This is very difficult because when you're very active you tend to forget about objectives and priorities.'[38]

Filtering out distractions

Jim Holbrook reasons as follows. 'You have to filter a lot of things out to stay focused on what's important. The way I look at it, the filtering mechanism is subconscious and automatic. The trick is to consciously set up the filters so that when you see something that is relevant and meaningful you can process it. All other things, you reject.'[39]

John Jamar warns against over-scheduling. 'If you've overloaded your schedule so you're at 120 per cent capacity, you'll tend to do the fun stuff first then go home,' he says. 'Then the tough stuff never gets done. Make sure you don't procrastinate on the tough stuff.'[40]

---

[38] Exclusive discussion with Thierry Grange, April 2008.
[39] Exclusive discussion with Jim Holbrook, March 2008.
[40] Exclusive discussion with John Jamar, March 2008.

Daniel Doimo adds his thoughts. 'We all tend to do pleasant things first and push the nasty things as far out as possible,' he says. 'The only way to overcome this is to have the discipline and the mental toughness to prioritize not on what's pleasant but on what's important. It's like doing push-ups in the morning. It might not be fun, but if you don't do it one day, the next day it is a little harder, and so on. You just have to bite the bullet and do it.'[41]

I asked Dan Packer what he thought about sticking to priorities. He went back to his experience during Hurricane Katrina. During the hurricane and the days just after, as CEO of the local energy company Dan had to set the right priorities and stick to them. He had to do this in spite of distractions. 'Our whole mission changed after the flooding,' he said. 'Our focus went from getting the lights back on to figuring out what we could do to get power to the water pumps. We also knew we had to get everybody out of the city. We needed to get the people off the roofs. And there were still the bad guys running around looting and taking advantage of people. We all had guns. Imagine that. We were all walking around the Hyatt with guns.'

'I went to the Superdome every day,' Dan said. 'I crossed that ramp going over from the Hyatt to the Superdome, and every day I saw this elderly woman dead in the water near the ramp. We couldn't get her. There wasn't anything we could do, so we just had to leave her there.'

'We were trying to get things done,' he said. 'There were a group of people who were hotel guests in the Hyatt. They did what we called 'vertical evacuation': they didn't leave town, they just went to a higher place. Every day they would go out and help rescue people from the rooftops.'

Dan continued: 'I was supposed to retire in December. There were a few things I had to get done first, and I was wrapping them up. But then came Katrina, so I had to stay on the job to take care of that. The financial analysts were saying the only way for Entergy to survive was to go bankrupt. We had no revenue for two weeks. Three weeks after the storm hit we declared bankruptcy.'

---

[41] Exclusive discussion with Daniel Doimo, March 2008.

'It's very eerie to be in a city with nobody,' he told me. 'There was just the military riding around with big guns. It was very strange. Fairly early on I went over to my own house to get a few things out. It hit me really hard to see all that damage. I felt bad flying around on the helicopter with people on the roof begging to be rescued. We were flying around to survey – to have a look. We knew the people would be rescued, but we couldn't do anything at the time.'

Dan said: 'In times like these you really have to stay focused. There is a natural tendency to go tend to your own house or to rescue people on the roofs. But had I done that I wouldn't have been taking care of the other important things. Far more people would have suffered had we not kept our eye on the big priorities.'[42]

Saying 'no'

Manuel Esquivel, former Prime Minister of Belize, points out: 'There are a multitude of issues competing for your time every day. You might want to do them all, but you just can't. So you have to prioritize. And you have to let people know if you can't give them your attention. Let them know and ask them to come back at another time. You just have to be up front and tell people "I will discuss it with you. But I can't do so immediately. Can we do it in three days?" If you make it clear you aren't just brushing them off, most people will accommodate that. This is a judgement you have to make. Only you can decide what your priorities are.'[43]

Manuel Esquivel was prime minister of Belize for a total of 10 years.

He says you have to find ways of saying 'no' firmly but politely. If you want to get things done, you have to get good at turning down opportunities that don't fit into your strategy.

Perhaps more important than choosing what to do is choosing what not to do. Opportunity cost is the loss you incur when you're doing one thing instead of another. You have lost the value of the thing you choose not to do. When you take on something new,

---

[42] Exclusive discussion with Dan Packer, October 2008.
[43] Exclusive discussion with Manuel Esquivel, June 2008.

make sure you understand what you'll have to stop doing to make time for the new task. Not only do you have to understand what to stop doing; you really have to stop doing it.

To drive this point home, consider what cognitive psychologists say about how much time we spend thinking about our different priorities. In a study by Eric Klinger and colleagues of the University of Minnesota, on average subjects reported devoting a third of their thoughts to a single priority and about half of their thinking to just two priorities (Klinger, Barta, and Maxeiner 1980).

Furthermore, Klinger (2008) says that when people become committed to pursuing a goal, 'that commitment sets in motion a powerful processing priority' causing goal-related thoughts to come to the foreground even at the cost of delaying other mental processing. Our thinking process limits us to working on very few important activities at a given time.

It's not worth trying to work against this natural boundary. Every time you agree to do something, you have to rule out something else. When you agree to do something you didn't really want to do, you might wind up squeezing out something you thought was important. It follows that turning things down is an integral part of good time management.

TIP #28

Learn to turn things down. If you aren't saying 'no' to opportunities, it probably means you have no strategy or direction.

James White puts it this way: 'Unless there are things you consistently say "no" to, you do not have a strategy. When given the opportunity to take something on, you need to evaluate it against your strategy. If it doesn't fit, then turn it down.'[44]

For Thierry Grange, 'saying "no" is sometimes the most difficult things to do, but it's frequently the wisest thing to do. We say sometimes that the moment you say "no" you have solved your problem.

---

[44] Exclusive discussion with James White, April 2008.

You are free. The moment you say "yes", that's when the mess starts. If you don't think you can sustain the effort needed to do something – or if you think you will lose motivation in the middle of doing it – it's better to say "no" right away and explain the reasons behind your refusal. A simple rule of thumb is: if it's not important for you, don't do it.'[45]

Manuel Perez de la Mesa is CEO of Pool Corp, a Fortune 1000 company with more than 3400 employees.

His view on time management: prioritise, prioritise, prioritise.

Manny Perez de la Mesa points out: 'You have a feeling about everything you do. Say "no" with empathy, but then you have to disengage emotionally. Don't sit around agonising about the fact you said "'no". Quickly move on to focus on what it is you really want to be doing.'[46]

Saying 'no' is not easy for most people. You have to be able to assess what's in line with your priorities and mission and you have to be able to say 'no' to all other things. When you say 'no' early, you're actually doing the other person a favour. If you say 'yes' or 'maybe' to something you really don't think is important, the chances are that you'll drop it in the end. You will have wasted your time and the other person's time.

What's also true is that if you can develop the habit of saying 'no' to things that aren't aligned with your mission, you communicate to people that you are selective. Then in the future when you do say 'yes' to something, they will place a higher value on your acceptance. They will know you're really behind it, because they know you're selective.

I asked Jim Whitehurst about saying 'no'. He told me about how companies suffer from this problem in the same way as individuals do. Jim said: 'More companies suffer from doing too much

---

[45] Exclusive discussion with Thierry Grange, April 2008.
[46] Exclusive discussion with Manuel Perez de la Mesa, March 2008.

than doing too little. It's harder than you think to stay focused. Everybody has some sort of pet project they want acceptance on. Saying 'no' is relatively hard, because you're making a choice. But implicitly you're also making a choice when you say 'yes'. You're making a choice to further disperse the efforts of the company.'

Jim went on to say: 'I think most companies suffer from what I call 'the shiny object syndrome'. You see a shiny object, so you want to go grab it. You rarely hear a company saying after the fact, "Gee, we focused too much on our core competencies and we wish we had done more different things!" I can't think of any case where a company regretted being focused.'

'On a personal level the same applies,' Jim said. 'On a personal level, it's also very easy to over-commit yourself. That's a habit you have to work hard to overcome, but it's a fundamental element of good time management.'[47]

Todd Davis told me: 'A lot of people handle whatever is in front of them at the moment, or whatever the squeaky wheel is. That's a losing approach. You don't stand a chance. People will learn that this is how you handle things and they will just line up to give you things to do. On the other hand if you come back and say "no", or redirect them, they'll understand what you're about and they'll know when to come to you and when not to come to you.'

'I learned the hard way how to say "no",' Todd said. 'Early in my career I was the young guy who wanted to show how much I could do. I was the first in the office and last to leave. Fortunately, I figured out that it was a losing battle.'

Todd continued: 'If they keep calling you to put out every fire, you're not going to be able to put out all the fires. You cannot win ever time. It was a losing proposition. It's not sustainable: the longer you do it, the less effective you are. It wears you out. I rethought my approach early in my career and decided to focus on doing the right things, rather than trying to do everything. This has worked much better for me.'[48]

---

[47] Exclusive discussion with Jim Whitehurst, April 2008.
[48] Exclusive discussion with Todd Davis, March 2008.

HABITS

For one week work on developing these two good habits.

Habit 5: Set very few priorities and stick to them

Select a maximum of two things that are your highest priority. Plan time to work on them, making sure the necessary resources are available when you need them. Be especially careful when those necessary resources are other people who have their own schedules.

Habit 6: Turn down things that are inconsistent with your priorities

Get used to the fact that there are many things you can't do. Learn to detach yourself quickly from things you decide not to do. Get good at saying 'no' to other people, and do so frequently.

How to work on habits

Here's a reminder of the procedure. In the morning think about the day's events that will allow you to reinforce these two habits. During the day take every opportunity to make them automatic. As a visual reminder, put this book, or a copy of this page, somewhere you can see it from time to time throughout the day. In the evening take five minutes to rate yourself on a scale of 1 to 5, with 1 indicating that you did very badly on the habit and 5 indicating that you did very well. Pencil in a rating for that day on the chart below.

HABIT	DAYS						
	1	2	3	4	5	6	7
Set very few priorities.							
Turn things down.							

EXERCISES

Here are some exercises to help you set priorities. The idea here is to sensitise you to the importance of making a conscious effort to prioritise and stay focused.

i   Given your list of WILL DO goals, without making a distinction between work goals and personal goals, rank them in order of importance to you. Be selfish here: don't confuse what's important to somebody else with what's important to you.

   a For each goal, note what you need to be doing now and in the near future to reach the goal.

   b Take the tasks together, regardless of which goal they are associated with, and order them by importance. Don't think about how much time each will take and don't think about how urgent each task is. Just think in terms of importance.

ii For each of your goals, write a rough plan to achieve it. Note whose help you need and when you need it.

iii If it's still early in the day, make a list of the five things you want to accomplish today. Otherwise, make a list for tomorrow. From time to time, have a look at that list to make sure you are staying focused on those things.

iv List the people you have trouble saying 'no' to, or situations in which you find it difficult to say 'no.' Think about why that is, and think about what you can do to change it. Find ways to practise saying 'no' to these people or in those situations.

v   For each of your WILL DO goals, think about things you'll have to turn down in order to stay focused on the goal. What distractions might come up? What new opportunities might come knocking? What people might demand your attention? Think of strategies for dealing with each of the things that might prevent you from accomplishing what you consider important.

7 OPTIMISE

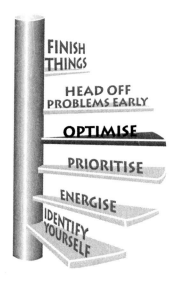

'Time management is an area you can never know enough about. It's a bit like sports. There's always something you can improve. If there are things you need to do now and will need to do in the future, try to get better at doing those things, just like you'd do in sports training. It makes a lot of sense to think of what things eat up your time and what you can do differently to alleviate that.' That's what Juha Christensen told me about optimising one's use of time.[1]

---

[1] Exclusive discussion with Juha Christensen, April 2008.

Juha has started several companies. He was one of the founders of Symbian, the company that developed the operating system powering hundreds of millions of mobile phones. He was also named one of the 25 most influential Europeans in high tech in Europe by *Time* magazine.

What are some good ways of doing things better and faster?

FOCUSED EFFORT

I once worked with a woman who thought she had this figured out. She managed a small team of quality assurance engineers, and she was responsible for finding all bugs in the firm's products before they were released. In the context of her job, it was appropriate to be somewhat of a perfectionist. And she was.

Anybody meeting her for the first time would think she was the most productive person in the company. She would set up two or three tests to run at the same time. And she let it be known it was okay to interrupt her and ask her to take a look at something. She wanted to be invited to all meetings, because she thought she needed to be on top of everything. And when she was in a meeting, she would keep her laptop running so that she could immediately look at any email that came in during the meeting.

Unfortunately her work wasn't making her happy. On top of that, while she might have appeared productive at first glance, she wasn't. Each of the tests she set up to run simultaneously required her attention. And people would interrupt her, because they knew they could. Constantly switching between tasks, she wound up giving very little of her attention to any given activity, and this showed up in the results. In meetings, because she was also working on email, she frequently had to ask people to go back over points she had missed. And often her messages didn't make sense – as if she hadn't really thought through what she was writing.

Her case is not unique. One thing we hear a lot about in the context of doing more things with less time is multitasking. Some people say that you can do several things at once – almost as if, by doing things simultaneously, you could somehow finish all of them faster than if you did them one at a time and in sequence. To some extent you do have to juggle different tasks, but multitasking is probably not the answer.

Myths on multitasking

Remember that the term 'multitasking' comes from the computer world. In the early days of the information age computers had only one processor, so a single computer could only execute one instruction at a time. Today most computers have several processors, allowing a given computer to execute several instructions simultaneously. To understand how computers multitask, let's just consider old-fashioned single-processor computers. After all, that's most analogous to the poor human being trying to juggle several tasks.

When several programs are vying for the services of a single CPU this is called 'multitasking'. The CPU can only really work on one thing at a time, but it has to distribute its time fairly among the different tasks. As we discussed in the last chapter, there are different strategies for allotting time to each activity. Now let's take a look at the overhead incurred each time a processor switches tasks.

Before allowing the processor to begin work on a new task, the operating system must first store the state of the current task for recall at a future point. Then it must load the state of the new task. This procedure is called 'context switching' – and as you may have guessed, it is pure overhead, because the processor does no useful work during the switch.

The amount of time allocated for each task to run is called a quantum. If an operating system is configured with a quantum of four milliseconds, and a context switch takes one millisecond, the computer will spend 20 per cent of its time context switching. In the extreme case where a computer is spending almost all of its time switching and very little time performing any one task, it's said to be 'thrashing'. Now consider a case where the quantum is set to 99 milliseconds, and the context switch takes one millisecond. Here the overhead of context switching will be minimal – only one per cent. However, when the quantum is set too high and the computer is servicing multiple users, all of whom request attention at the same time, some users will perceive a delay.

People who design and configure operating systems have to make a tradeoff between optimising overall CPU usage and minimising the delay experienced by users.

People managing their own time have to make a similar tradeoff. They may be in a situation in which they have to respond quickly to a lot of different people, but then the overhead of context switching gets out of hand. One key difference between a person and a computer is that the computer can switch context with 100 per cent accuracy, whereas human beings lose information each time they stop one task to start work on another. On each switch, a computer loses time but not information, whereas a person loses both.

TIP #29

When a computer multitasks it loses time switching between tasks, but it never loses information. When people multitask they lose both time and information.

Sometimes you can't avoid dealing with a multitude of interruptions. It might be the nature of your job. In this case, there are some techniques that can help you switch context more smoothly and lose less information in the process.

Janice Chaffin, who has been working in the computer industry for decades, probably quite naturally adopted a procedure of switching between tasks that is similar to an operating system's context switching. When I discussed the overhead of multitasking with her, she told me: 'The nature of my job is such that I have to deal with hundreds of different things every day. I might start on one activity, and just after starting I get interrupted and move on to something else. I now know that to keep on track I need to write things down. Once a week I go back to these notes to make sure I've covered everything.'[2]

Les Hirsch does this kind of thing when going from one meeting to another. 'As CEO you have to switch from one task to another

---

[2] Exclusive discussion with Janice Chaffin, March 2008.

without missing a step,' he told me. 'One thing that works for me is, when possible, to take just a minute or so to think about what you are about to do. On the walk to where I'm going I think a lot about what I am going to say at the meeting or during the presentation. That walk is a ritual that gives me a couple of minutes to prepare. I think about who I'm meeting, what we're trying to accomplish, and what are the issues.'[3]

Ray Titus of United Franchise Group reckons that 'there are some cases where you need to multitask, but not when you're dealing with people. There should be no multitasking when you're developing a relationship with somebody. You need to pay full attention to the person you're dealing with. What's more, I've read studies that show the employee who's been smoking marijuana has more brain power than the employee who's multitasking.'[4]

According to the CEO of Redknee, 'Multitasking is an illusion you live through when you are really young.' Lucas Skoczkowski, who at 35 is still young for a CEO, goes on to say: 'We are big users of BlackBerry devices in my company. But I have barred their use during meetings. I tell people that if they're multitasking, it's likely their IQ is half of what it should be in my meeting. There has been research on multitasking where psychologists measured IQ. These studies demonstrate that your ability to be effective per unit of time goes down. You might harbor the illusion that you're getting a lot done, but you'll probably be frustrated and feel overwhelmed in the end. You have made very ineffective use of your time.'[5]

Another young CEO, Jim Whitehurst, the 40-year-old CEO of Red Hat, told me: 'This idea of doing your email while you're on the phone, or using your BlackBerry during a meeting, is extraordinarily inefficient. I'm all for making use of dead time, such as when you're waiting in line at the airport or exercising in a gym. But there I'm talking about time where your mind is not required to be in two places at once.'

'I insist that people close laptops and not use BlackBerries during meetings,' Jim says. 'Because when you get right down to it,

---

[3] Exclusive discussion with Les Hirsch, March 2008.
[4] Exclusive discussion with Ray Titus, July 2008.
[5] Exclusive discussion with Lucas Skoczkowski, April 2008.

you aren't really being that thoughtful on your laptop or your BlackBerry and you aren't paying attention to the meeting either. In the end you're doing both badly.'

Jim Whitehurst started his career as a software engineer. Barely 40 years old, he has made a name for himself as somebody who gets things done: he did this as COO of Delta Airlines, and now as CEO of Red Hat.

Jim thinks the idea of multitasking as a way of getting more done is ridiculous. He says you're much more effective when you do one thing at a time.

And, according to Jim, even when you're on the phone, the other person can get irritated if you're doing something other than participating in the conversation. 'You can tell when you're on a call with somebody and they're simultaneously doing something on their computer. They might say something, but it's almost like they're saying something to prove they're listening. They wind up not being very useful on the call. On top of that, I'm sure they aren't doing a very good job with whatever it is they're doing on the computer. It's a waste of time.'

Jim Whitehurst summarised his feeling about multitasking. 'I think this idea that multitasking saves time is ridiculous.'[6]

Former prime minister of Belize Manuel Esquivel told me: 'I find it extremely frustrating when I'm doing something and get interrupted. Because if I switch to something else, each of the two tasks takes twice as long as they normally would. I really do prefer to complete one thing and then move on to the next. It doesn't mean I solve all problems right away. It means I reach a completion point, or a point at which I've solved my part of the problem.'

'When you can't complete something in one sitting,' Manuel continued 'you can still reach a completion point. You can divide the problem into chunks and do one chunk at a time. This makes it easier to

---

[6] Exclusive discussion with Jim Whitehurst, April 2008.

go back and work on the rest of the problem. And you get a sense of satisfaction when you've reached a completion point – or especially when you've solved the problem.'[7]

Lucas Skoczkowski agrees. He says: 'You have to take bigger blocks of time and fend off interruptions as you focus your effort during that time. Interruptions cause suboptimal performance. You don't have enough time to get into what you're doing. You feel you're busy, but you also feel a lot of stress and you get a sense of being overwhelmed. Switching context is fairly high overhead, whether you like it or not.'[8]

Minimising distraction

Indeed, you need to spend a sufficient chunk of time on each task and give it enough focus to move it forward. And you should look for good stopping points that allow you to switch smoothly to a second activity without worrying about what you left behind. The clean stopping point will also help you get back to work on the first task later.

Serial entrepreneur Scott Goldman said: 'I find it much more efficient to compartmentalise and block off time for focused effort. This works better than doing a little email, having a bite to eat, talking on the phone a little, and simultaneously reading a little. I do realise that in today's world you have to multitask to some extent. However, given the opportunity, I try to silo tasks and do them in isolation.'[9]

Janice Chaffin, president of the consumer group at Symantec, told me, 'It's frustrating when you can't find uninterrupted time to get things done. This is especially true when you need to do strategic thinking. You cannot do five minutes here, five minutes there. You need to have focused effort. What I have done for years and years is create 'protected time' by blocking a three- or four-hour time slot on my calendar at some time during the week. In my case it happens to be Friday morning. That seems to work reasonably well. I try to use that time for catch-up, writing reviews, strategic thinking, or just anything I need to do without interruption. I don't get those

---

[7] Exclusive discussion with Manuel Esquivel, June 2008.
[8] Exclusive discussion with Lucas Skoczkowski, April 2008.
[9] Exclusive discussion with Scott Goldman, March 2008.

every week, because things come up. But most weeks it works out. It really relieves the frustration, because you get things finished before the weekend.'[10]

Jim Whitehurst adds, 'It's very difficult not to think of all the things you want to do. Sometimes they cloud the mind and confuse your focus. I can assure you, if you can eliminate these kinds of distractions and really focus, you will be far more successful in accomplishing whatever it is you're trying to achieve.'[11]

I like the way the CEO of Integrys Energy Services sums it up. Mark Radtke says: 'Most of what I do to manage my time is oriented to maintaining focus.'[12]

MAKING TIME

No matter where I go, somebody always comes up to me and talks about how they simply can't fit something into their schedule. I'm always amazed by people who don't seem to have a lot to do, and yet can't find time to do anything new.

One example that stands out is a university science professor who contacted me to talk about one of my articles on time management. This particular article was on the subject of meetings – a topic that was interesting to the professor, because his work meetings seemed to be big time wasters. He told me the meetings he chaired would always run over time and he never could cover all he wanted to. Somehow his meetings were always derailed.

We agreed to get together for lunch. Our discussion went on and on, without really covering the essential points he contacted me about. It occurred to me that this might be his problem. He was diluting the conversation so much that it was a real effort to listen to him and filter out the junk to get to what he was trying to say.

The professor wasn't asking for advice, so I didn't give him any. He simply wanted to talk in a theoretical way about time management. Still, I related some anecdotes, hoping he'd spot some

---

[10] Exclusive discussion with Janice Chaffin, March 2008.
[11] Exclusive discussion with Jim Whitehurst, April 2008.
[12] Exclusive discussion with Mark Radtke, April 2008.

similarities with his own struggles. It turns out that the problem he had was exactly like what Manuel Esquivel told me about people not getting to the point.

Eliminating unnecessary steps

Several years ago Manuel Esquivel was the prime minister of Belize. Now he is senior advisor to the current prime minister. He has also been head of his political party. Needless to say, throughout his career he has had to deal with a lot of people. 'I find that the most time is wasted listening to people who take 15 minutes to get to the point, or reading reports that are 100 pages long,' he said. 'I tell people to make sure they have something to say – make sure they have it sorted out in their mind and let me know what it is. I tell people to keep reports down to around three pages long. A lot of times people write a very long document and they get lost in it and forget what they're trying to say. When you're dealing with a lot of people, especially in a political environment, they tend to tell you their whole life story before they get to the point. You just have to interrupt and ask them in a kind way to get to the point.'[13]

Just how important is getting to the point? One of the most successful businessmen of our times, Michael Dell, has practically based his life on the idea of cutting out unnecessary steps. This philosophy was the basis for his company's success in its early years. But even before that – much earlier in his life – he made a rather spectacular attempt to use this idea to his advantage. When he was in the third grade he applied to take a test to get his high school diploma. Much to his parents' surprise, he had a woman from the testing company come to his house to talk to him about how he could take just one test to get a high school diploma. Dell's thinking was that he could eliminate the nine remaining school years! (Dell with Fredman 1999)

Finding out where you spend your time

Ray Titus provides these thoughts on getting more done: 'We have 1400 franchisees in 50 different countries around the world working within our five different brands. One of the things we do to maximise our success is train franchise owners. We train them to

---

[13] Exclusive discussion with Manuel Esquivel, June 2008.

become successful entrepreneurs. Because our success ultimately depends on their success, we do what we can to make sure they do well.'

Ray enlightened me with an example of an exercise they use during training. 'A very simple thing we have our franchisers do during training is, for one day, [to] note everything they do and how long it takes,' Ray said. 'When you look at this the next day, you get a surprising view of how much time you waste. That's one thing few people do. It's a big eye opener.'[14]

In my own training programmes I provide a technique for getting an objective view of where you spend your time. It works as follows. Over a three-day period note down everything you do that takes more than five minutes. You don't have to be exact. You might not be able to write down things as they happen. Instead, most people I train stop at noon and think about what they did over the last three hours. This is accurate enough.

At the end of the three days, put it all on paper or in a spread-sheet. This will give you a good view of where you spend your time. Once you see this, you can look for activities you might eliminate. In cases where there's nothing you can do about wasted time, you might look for ways of making the best use of the dead time.

To illustrate this technique, Table 7.1 shows an excerpt from one of my three days. This is not the first time I've gone through this exercise, so I had already made some improvements in how I or-ganise my day. For example, I had learned to do my email only at certain times during the day. I had learned to block off time for focused effort in the morning, and to make most of my phone calls in the afternoon.

In this excerpt you can see there were two periods when my motivation dropped off – at around 2:00 p.m., and again at around 3:30 p.m. The drop at 2:00 p.m. is the result of having eaten a heavy lunch and having had two glasses of wine. The drop at 3:30 p.m.

---

[14] Exclusive discussion with Ray Titus, July 2008.

Table 7.1 An excerpt from my record of the way I spent a day

START TIME	END TIME	ACTIVITY
7:00	7:15	*Coffee/breakfast*
7:15	7:30	*Shower and dress*
7:30	8:05	*Drive kids to school*
8:05	8:25	*Email*
8:25	8:30	*Write top five list and schedule day*
8:30	10:30	*Work on book*
10:30	10:45	*Call IPW*
10:45	11:00	*Email*
11:00	12:00	*Work on book*
12:00	14:00	*Lunch with friends; goofing off; two glasses of wine*
14:00	14:20	*Don't feel like doing anything*
14:20	15:30	*Cold call training companies*
15:30	16:05	*No motivation; not sure what to do*
16:05	17:10	*Distracted and browsing the web with no purpose*

is because I had done cold calling just before. Whenever you have to call people you don't know and try to set up a partnership, you're likely to feel deflated afterwards. This is a natural consequence of being rejected several times in a row.

Thanks to this exercise I gain an objective view of where I spend my time, and I can make choices accordingly. I might decide to continue having heavy lunches and drinking wine with lunch from time to time, or I might decide never to do that. At least I know the consequences of my choice. One change I made was to schedule 20 minutes of exercise after cold calls. This picks me up and allows me to segue into something else.

Once you get this view of where you spend your time, you can look for periods when you were distracted, and you can look for cases where you can piggyback. Piggybacking means knocking out several activities while you're in town or at the grocery store. But it also means grouping things by context. Instead of writing email right away when you think of doing it, keep a list of messages you want to send. Then block off two or three email sessions during the day. During those sessions go through your list and do them all.

The idea is to group things by context so that you can knock them all out while in the appropriate mindset. Examples of different contexts you might be in during a given day include:

- talking to a particular client;
- talking to the boss;
- doing email;
- at the grocery store;
- driving into town;
- making phone calls.

Once you have an objective view, you might find activities you can eliminate altogether. Or, where you feel you're wasting your time but you just can't avoid it, you might look for ways of filling the dead time.

Making use of dead time

Jim Whitehurst of Red Hat told me he likes to find ways of making good use of time that's normally wasted. 'There's a lot of time during the day that's potentially wasted, or dead time,' he said. 'For example, you might be driving into work, waiting in the security line at the airport, or working out. You have to find ways of making that time useful.'

TIP #30

Take notes on what you do over a period of several days. Spot ways in which you waste time, and cut out those activities wherever you can. Look for ways of filling remaining dead time with useful activity.

Jim said: 'For environmental reasons I like to fly commercial, rather than private. When I'm in the security line at the airport I might call two or three people, or I might do email on my BlackBerry. After I get through security, I go to where I need to be. Then I find as quiet a place as possible and sit down to get some work done.'

As for getting stuff done while exercising at home, Jim says: 'I bought a special stand for my laptop so I can clean out email in the morning while I'm working out on the treadmill. When I go to a gym I might print something out to read while exercising, or I might read the newspaper to keep up on what's happening in the world.'

Jim summarises: 'It's important to think through how you can use dead time to your advantage. The choice comes down to either getting busy doing something useful or wasting your time staring at walls.'[15]

Serial entrepreneur Scott Goldman has a few neat tricks that help him. 'I keep a stack of trade journals I don't normally have the time to go through on a small desk,' he said. 'When I have a spare moment, I go through those trade journals and rip out the material I find relevant. I put those pages in a folder for later. When I'm on a flight or waiting in an airport, or just not doing anything, I'll reach for that folder and read through those articles.'

Among other things, Scott was the first CEO of the WAP Forum, the organisation that set the first standards for browsing the web from a mobile phone. Scott shares another time saver:

---

[15] Exclusive discussion with Jim Whitehurst, April 2008.

'There are several podcasts I'm interested in. What I do is have those automatically downloaded and then listen to them later in the car.'[16]

TIPS AND TRICKS

According to Daniel Doimo of APC by Schneider, 'The only way you get better is by doing something beyond your ability. You have to take on a challenge. If you are able to constantly challenge yourself, and do things that are not easy, you stand a good chance of gaining a competitive advantage. And when you take on a challenge, you just have to dig in and do the work required. When you decide to ride your bike up a mountain, the decision itself might be easy. But then you have to go out and do it. You have to deliver on that promise to yourself. In doing so, the next time you make that decision, you do so knowing you're really going to do it.'[17]

Peter Wildhorn agrees. The CEO of IPW Group, a company that manufactures circuit boards in China, says: 'Spend a little time every day trying to get better at things you do regularly. You can do this by figuring out shortcuts. And you can do this by pushing yourself beyond your limit.'[18]

Let's look at some ways to increase inefficiency in a few everyday situations.

Reading
We all have a lot to read every day. There are two ways of getting through all that information faster: read faster or learn to skim quickly over information you don't need in order to get to what you do need.

Scott Goldman is technically minded by nature. To stay on top of things, he has to take in a lot of information quickly. So I asked him if he had any tips on reading.

---

[16] Exclusive discussion with Scott Goldman, March 2008.
[17] Exclusive discussion with Daniel Doimo, March 2008.
[18] Exclusive discussion with Peter Wildhorn, March 2008.

The 'Wireless Wizard', Scott Goldman, was the first CEO of the WAP Forum, the organisation that defined the standards for web browsing from mobile phones and personal digital assistants. He has started and run several companies.

When he reads, Scott skims over the text until he gets to the heart of the matter. He reads that part several times. We get so much information these days that when you read you have to home in on what's important – and then be sure to really understand that part.

'The first thing I do is discriminate what I read,' Scott said. 'I try to judge carefully what I decide to read, by looking at the title, some of the headlines, and the author. Over time, I get to know some of the authors and publications I like.'

He continued, 'I read pretty fast, but what helps most is that I have trained myself to quickly get to the material that interests me. The biggest problem in reading is that many people try to absorb all details when they are really only interested in certain parts of the article or book. I approach reading like a heat-seeking missile, where I skim over parts that don't interest me to home in on the parts I'm after. When I find these parts, I slow down and read them carefully. I may read those parts three, four, or five times just to make sure I fully understand the critical material.'[19]

Meetings
If you are working in a group, you have to assemble people to share information and make decisions. You need to get people on the same page, and then to move forward in concert. But meetings can be a huge time waster.

On this subject, Janice Chaffin told me: 'I'm constantly looking for ways of making meetings more efficient. I like my staff meetings to be times for decision making, but since my team is spread out around the world, I usually have to take the time to disseminate information so everybody is on the same page. This is a necessary prerequisite to decision making. If attendees do not have the same

---

[19] Exclusive discussion with Scott Goldman, March 2008.

perception of the situation, you can't make informed decisions. In my case, because my team is so spread out geographically, I have to mix information sharing with decision making. I suppose this is true to some extent for most staff meetings. It just varies by degree. Given that fact of life, I'm always looking for the optimal mix of the two for meetings I control.'[20]

The former CEO of Extended Systems, one of the first market leaders in mobile software products, Steve Simpson considers meetings a necessary evil.

There's value in holding regular meetings, but make sure they don't take on a life of their own. If you don't watch out, internal meetings will grow like cancer in your company, eating up everybody's time.[21]

'Acute meetingitis' is what Gilles du Chaffaut refers to as the tendency to have meetings just for the sake of having meetings. 'It seems to me that after about an hour and a half of meeting time you reach the point of diminishing returns,' according to Gilles, the city manager of Grenoble, France. 'Meetings should last a set amount of time that's decided in advance. The purpose of the meeting should be clear to all those invited, exactly the people who need to be there should be there, and the meeting should have an outcome. Usually having an outcome means something gets decided.'

He went on to say: 'You also need to write notes on the meeting. If you don't write minutes and share them with all those involved, you may have wasted your time. Every attendee will have his or her own interpretation of the encounter, which defeats the whole purpose of coming together to act in concert. The minutes should summarise the main points and should list what was decided and any actions to be taken along with the name of the person responsible for taking the action.'[22]

---

[20] Exclusive discussion with Janice Chaffin, March 2008.
[21] Exclusive discussion with Steve Simpson, March 2008.
[22] Exclusive discussion with Gilles du Chaffaut, November 2008.

The checklist in Figure 7.1 summarises this advice about meetings.

Figure 7.1 Meeting checklist

Meeting Checklist

✓ *Invite only those people who must attend, and nobody else.*

✓ *Publish the agenda well in advance.*

✓ *Plan no more than one-and-a-half hours for the meeting.*

✓ *Start on time and end on time.*

✓ *Stick to the agenda.*

✓ *If you get stuck on a point, make a decision about how to resolve it outside the meeting.*

✓ *Summarise action items at the end of the meeting.*

✓ *Publish meeting notes and follow up on actions.*

You might also try to keep meetings very short. Juha Christensen told me: 'My day is full of a lot of short meetings, 15 or 30 minutes long, and rarely up to two or three hours. I like short meetings. I'm a big believer in the idea that you can achieve just as much in a 15-minute meeting as you can in a one-hour meeting, so I have a lot of 15-minute meetings. I don't like a lot of interruptions. But I always promise people they can have a 15-minute meeting with me, given a few hours notice. If they want an hour meeting, they can get it with a day's notice. If they need longer than that, they can get it with a few days' notice. That's to make sure I don't suffer from death by a thousand cuts. The things people tend to drop by for are rarely important issues. They mostly have the urgent issues. In most cases, it's stuff they could figure out themselves. The more position power you have, the more you have to look out for this potential time waster.'

Email
Even though he's led high-tech companies all his adult life, Juha warns against getting carried away with technology. 'I think you have to limit email,' he says. 'Email is evil. You can sit down and just go on and on with email. The more you send, the more that gets generated. You just get stuck. I try to have two to three chunks of email time a day. I'm pretty careful about that. I might also do email here and there, like if I'm stuck in traffic. But I'm not a fan of checking messages during meetings. It tends to draw too much attention away. The BlackBerry is great for when you have pockets of time when you are free to check mail.'[23]

Jean-René Bouvier is CEO of Buzzinbees, offering software that runs in wireless network infrastructure to help operators run pre-pay services. Before that, he was vice-president at HP in charge of HP's billion-dollar business developing signalling software to allow networks to provide all the fancy services we now take for granted.

Jean-René doesn't let incoming email accumulate to more than two pages of unread messages. When it gets to that point, he knows it's time to clear it out.[24]

But some people have jobs that require they be responsive. Take for example Brit Kirwan, Chancellor of the University of Maryland, who says: 'Being accessible to people has been an important aspect of my management style. If people want to send me a message or write me a letter, they might get a short response, but it

---

[23] Exclusive discussion with Juha Christensen, April 2008.
[24] Exclusive discussion with Jean-René Bouvier, April 2010.

will be a courteous response pointing them in the right direction. I take pride in being responsive. Some people might think this is not good time management – that it's a waste of time in the short term. On the other hand, I think there is some kind of overall long-term benefit – particularly to somebody in my kind of role – to being seen as somebody responsive and connected to the various constituents.'[25]

Gilles du Chaffaut says messages shouldn't be too long. The city manager of Grenoble, France says: 'When a message is too long, say over a page, you're probably better off talking with the person on the phone or meeting in person. The other problem I find with email is when you copy a whole lot of people who aren't really involved – and especially when you don't make it clear you're expecting a response from somebody. If you want a response, you should be clear what the question is and who should respond. Some people have come to me and asked why I didn't answer a message I was just copied on. I simply do not have infinite capacity to react to email.'[26]

Telephone

When discussing productivity tools, we can't take the phone for granted. John Jamar runs CCI Systems, which is a service-oriented company. As such, they have to be responsive. John says: 'I try to keep my response time to email and phone calls down to two hours. This keeps me in a service-oriented mode, it's partner and customer friendly, and it get things out of the way quicker.'[27]

Similarly, a lot of John Koerner's success comes from building good relationships. Among other things, he was King of Mardi Gras in 2008. To build good relationships you have to stay in touch and get back to people. He says: 'I return all phone calls by sunset. I try to return even the distasteful calls quickly just to get them over with.'[28]

On using the phone, Scott Goldman shared the following with me: 'I try to prepare for each phone call. If you take a minute before each phone call to think about the goals of the call, you

---

[25] Exclusive discussion with William Kirwan, May 2008.
[26] Exclusive discussion with Gilles du Chaffaut, November 2008.
[27] Exclusive discussion with John Jamar, March 2008.
[28] Exclusive discussion with John Koerner, June 2008.

can make your participation in the call more effective. I usually block off a little extra time at the end. If the call needs to go on longer I can accommodate. If it doesn't then I can use that time for follow-up and I can use it as a sort of slush fund to do other activities I've set aside.'[29]

Ray Titus cautions not to let the phone keep you from doing what you think is important. He says, 'People are too accessible. Employees carry their cell phones wherever they go and they get text messages or phone calls all the time. This is a distraction. Furthermore, when you're too accessible you're at the whim of the other person. You fall victim to the other person's time management. You're doing what they want you to do – not what you want to do. The other person is getting something done, but you're not. You're on the defensive. You certainly should help people, but not at the expense of getting done what you need to get done. Be careful not to fall into the trap of working on their to-do list at the expense of your own.'

In summary, he says: 'If you're at somebody else's beck and call, there's no way you can do what you want.'[30]

Electronic calendars
The top five list we discussed in the previous chapter is a useful way of keeping track of what's important. If you develop the habit of noting things that are important, you no longer have to think about those things when you aren't working on them. You can take this a step further by using a calendar. Take a moment in the morning to allocate time to work on each of the things you want to move forward. By doing so, you free yourself to think only about what you are doing now.

Listen to what Mark Radtke says. According to the CEO of Integrys Energy Services, 'Electronic calendaring is a very useful technology. It allows you to maintain a tight schedule. My entire day is scheduled. If I have a meeting, I schedule not only the meeting, but also the time before to prepare, and time after for follow-up activity.'[31]

---

[29] Exclusive discussion with Scott Goldman, March 2008.
[30] Exclusive discussion with Ray Titus, July 2008.
[31] Exclusive discussion with Mark Radtke, April 2008.

Jean-René Bouvier of Buzzinbees doesn't just use his calendar to schedule meetings with other people – he also schedules things he does alone. If he's planning to exercise, that goes in his calendar; if he needs to work on something alone, that goes in his calendar.[32]

Serial entrepreneur Juha Christensen even schedules time to goof off. He says that it's important to leave time just to do nothing. Why not put that in your schedule, so you know you've allocated time for it?[33]

DELEGATING

You don't have time to do everything yourself – and you also don't have the skills to do it all – so you have to know what to delegate and to whom. Depending on your situation you may delegate to subordinates, to peers, or to higher ups. This is true in work and it's true in your personal life.

> Gary Heavin started Curves with his wife, Diane. The fastest growing franchise ever, Curves was built by word of mouth, and by making sure that everybody involved benefits.
>
> Gary spends a lot of time building trusting relationships. Once you establish trust in both directions and share common values, delegating in either direction is no problem at all.[34]

Remember that when you ask somebody to do something, you're asking them to accept the importance of the task. How they internalise the importance or the value of the task makes all the difference in how well they perform. Psychologist Edward Deci (1995) talks about three things that can happen when you try to get somebody to internalise an idea. These are **rejection** (they don't accept the idea at all), **introjection** (they accept it superficially but not

---

[32] Exclusive discussion with Jean-René Bouvier, April 2010.

[33] Exclusive discussion with Juha Christensen, April 2008.

[34] Exclusive discussion with Gary Heavin, April 2010.

wholeheartedly, much like swallowing something without digesting it), and **integration** (they fully accept the idea it as if it were their own).

Deci's experiments on getting somebody to do a boring task show that if three elements are present in the demand, the subject is more likely to integrate the task, as demonstrated by the fact that they perform the activity in their free time. They will take on the job and show volition if the demand includes these elements:

- providing a rationale;
- acknowledging that it may be something they do not want to do;
- granting that they do have a choice about not doing it, while at the same time emphasising that it's important to you that they do it.

In practice it's not so hard to provide a rationale and to acknowledge that it's not something they want to do. However, giving the other person a choice not to perform the task is not always something you want to do when delegating downwards. You won't achieve perfection here – just do the best you can to try to include these three elements when asking somebody to do something for you. If you can minimise the pressure – and thereby give the other person some sense of choice – he or she will take ownership of the task and will do a better job of it.

Delegating to somebody

On delegating, Patrick Quinlan told me: 'When you're running an organisation of any size, you want to spread out the work to approach the definition of efficiency, which is **each doing only what each can do**. When people aren't doing the job they're supposed to be doing, that will eventually bubble up to the CEO. In this situation, people, starting with the CEO, aren't delegating appropriately. To delegate requires clear direction, and proper recruitment and training. It's all about getting other people to do their jobs, so you don't have to do it for them.'[35]

---

[35] Exclusive discussion with Patrick Quinlan, April 2008.

TIP #31

When asking somebody to do something for you, the better you communicate the rationale behind your request, the more the other person will feel a sense of choice in taking it on – and consequently, the better the other person will perform the work.

Juha Christensen warns against wasting time following up on things that were never important in the first place. He says: 'Delegating is one of those things that make the difference between a good leader and a not so good leader. Good leaders are ruthless at handing off urgent but unimportant tasks to somebody else and not feeling the need to follow up to see if it's completed. If it's not important, why should you have to follow up on it? Avoid that urge.'[36]

Dan Packer does what Edward Deci's experiments have shown to be optimal. The former CEO of Entergy says: 'I don't just go charging in. My approach has always been to give them all the information I have and see if they can reach the same conclusion I've come to. That doesn't mean I won't come out in the end and say "that's what you ought to be doing right now" or "that's what I want you to do", but it's better if they say that before I get a chance to. It's best to give them all the information I have, give them the options I see, and try to get to the point where it's either their idea or it's something they want to do. It might take a little more time to delegate this way, but that extra investment up front has a big payoff.'

'Folks will understand what you're trying to do,' Dan says. 'Some will try to wait it out until I tell them what to do – and usually those are the people who need to be told what to do in the first place. But it doesn't hurt to walk them through step by step so they understand the rationale anyway.'

Dan goes on to say: 'There are some times when you have to delegate something to somebody and you know the person doesn't want to do it. That doesn't change your approach. You still have to give them all the information you have. They'll usually come to the

---

[36] Exclusive discussion with Juha Christensen, April 2008.

conclusion that even though they don't want to do it, it's acceptable. They understand the reasoning, and they appreciate having been given all the information available.'[37]

For Suri of American Reprographics, it's important to learn to give up work and let others do it. He says: 'On a daily basis I look at the work in front of me and ask myself, is this something I can have done by somebody else? And if it is something I can hand off, do I have the people who can get it done? As American Reprographics has grown from being a nine-million-dollar company to almost a one-billion-dollar company with 5200 people, I have had to change the kinds of things I do, and the kinds of things I delegate. This involves progressively letting go of a lot of things. I have to make sure I'm delegating effectively, and then holding people accountable after that.'[38]

Jean-René Bouvier has a set of rules he uses for delegating. He used them when he managed a billion-dollar business within HP, and he uses them now as CEO of Buzzinbees. His rules are shown in Figure 7.2.[39]

The CEO of Energizer Holdings, Ward Klein, advises anybody in a management role to pick good people and delegate. Give them authority and responsibility, and hold them accountable. Give them the space they need to do their jobs, and don't do their jobs for them. He says he has taken that approach over the years.

'This does a couple of things,' Ward explains. 'First it frees me up to focus on other strategic issues, not necessarily tactical implementation. Second it allows me to focus on one of my key jobs, which is picking the right people for the right jobs. By delegating responsibilities and holding people accountable, you set up a clear process for developing really good executives under you.'

Ward says: 'The stronger the people who work under me, the more freedom I have to attend to what I have to get done. In my case, that management style has helped me do a lot.'[40]

---

[37] Exclusive discussion with Dan Packer, October 2008.
[38] Exclusive discussion with K. Surivakumar (Suri), March 2008.
[39] Exclusive discussion with Jean-René Bouvier, April 2010.
[40] Exclusive discussion with Ward Klein, March 2008.

Figure 7.2 Rules for delegating

Rules for Delegating

✓ *When you don't know your team yet, delegate progressively by giving short deadlines on lesser items. This allows you to determine who you can trust and who you must coach.*

✓ *Delegate bigger and longer tasks as fast as possible to those you can trust. This will motivate them and free up time.*

✓ *Coach others and also allocate them tasks they are better fit for in order to fully utilise your team. Resist the temptation to work only with the highest performers.*

✓ *Constantly monitor the motivation and desire of the top performers and encourage them to move to new jobs and leave you. This will attract other top performers to your team and create a network of former teammates that will help you from outside.*

Paul Kruse is CEO of Blue Bell Creameries, the number one vendor of ice cream in the southern United States.

He says: 'There are so many things I want to do, and I might be good at many of those things, but I have no business doing them. Other people will get a lot of satisfaction from doing it, and they will do it well, so the best thing for me to do is give it to those other people. It also frees me up to do the job I'm supposed to do, which is overseeing things instead of trying to do them myself.'[41]

---

[41] Exclusive discussion with Paul Kruse, March 2008.

According to John Jamar, 'Frequently, when people are having problems delegating, it's not because they're bad delegators. It's because they have doubts about the decision-making capabilities of those delegated to.'

'If I know what you believe and I know that you understand our corporate culture,' he elaborated, 'I have a lot more trust in how you will make a decision. I therefore have an easier time delegating. This allows us to push the decision making to the person closest to the problem. Consequently the organisation is more responsive.'[42]

It's important to be good at delegating, but it's also important to think about how you accept tasks delegated to you. Accepting work in the most efficient manner possible is good time management.

Having something delegated to you
A woman who attended my training told me she felt overwhelmed at work. A support engineer, she always had something to work on, but people frequently came up to her and asked her to do other things. This could be her boss, her boss's boss, or it could be a peer. She lost all sense of choice. She felt that she was at the mercy of anybody who came along and asked her to do something. We worked out some ways she could regain the sense of choice, and at the same time make it clear to other people that she wasn't automatically going to say 'yes'.

Whenever you're in the position of being asked to do something for somebody else – whether that other person is a boss, a peer, or an underling – it's important to communicate to the other person that you can choose not to do it. They'll respect you much more in the long run. And you'll feel better about taking on what they ask you to do.

You don't want to appear unwilling to help. But you do want to make sure you understand their reasoning. And you want to make it clear that it's important for you to understand what they're asking you to do and why they're asking you, of all people. Depending on who's delegating to you, there are different ways of doing this.

---

[42] Exclusive discussion with John Jamar, March 2008.

- **With a boss** ask questions so as to understand the reasons for doing the task. Make sure you don't appear to be questioning your boss's judgement. Your questions should be designed to help you develop your own understanding of how this particular task fits into an overall plan.

- **With a peer** ask questions so as to understand what he or she is trying to achieve and how this particular task fits into an overall plan. Also ask questions to find out why you are the one who should do the task.

- **With an underling** ask questions so as to understand why the person can't do the task without you.

No matter how you are positioned in an organisation, there's always somebody who will try to give you something to do. Work doesn't always flow from the top down. As Gary Stockman of Porter Novelli told me, 'People tend to think delegating is something that occurs in the downward direction only, but that's not true. There are some people who are very masterful at delegating up – at handing things up to their boss. "I need approval for this" or "I was hoping you could help me with that", they might say. Sometimes this is legitimate, but sometimes they are trying to shirk responsibility. It's important to say "no" when this is done inappropriately.'[43]

As for having something delegated to you from a boss, if the boss is particularly awkward – or downright abusive – you have to handle the situation with care. The former CEO of Entergy New Orleans, Dan Packer, illustrates this point through experiences he had in dealing with his own bosses throughout his career. 'Sometimes you will have somebody delegating things to you in a heavy-handed manner,' he told me. 'You have to ask yourself how much time and energy you want to put into trying to change somebody who probably can't be changed. Sometimes you have to try to go with it anyway in hopes that once he or she gets to know you, they'll adjust their delegation style.'

'On the other hand, I had one boss who was really rough,' Dan said. 'He was kind of a big guy. He would lean into you and try to

---

[43] Exclusive discussion with Gary Stockman, March 2008.

intimidate you into doing something you were already going to do anyway. I came to a point where I couldn't take it any more and I decided to confront him on this before the problem got worst. I told him, "You're the boss. If you tell me to do something, I'm going to do it. But if you stand over me and whip me, I'm going to take that whip from you and whip you back." I meant this in a figurative sense, of course. He understood what I was saying and changed. He started to give me a lot more information and was more sincere than in the past.'

'It worked that time,' Dan continued. 'Being direct like that doesn't always work. With other abusive bosses, I knew I couldn't take that approach. They wouldn't fire me or anything like that, but I wouldn't get anywhere with their help. They were intimidating, but they could be easily intimidated themselves. I had to be careful if I wanted them to help me in some way. They would have reasoned "I'm not going to help this guy. He came back at me once. I'll stay away from him." Sometimes the right thing to do is confront the person. Sometimes it's not. You have to feel it out.'

Dan told me about another case. 'I had a different boss who was heavy handed. I thought about confronting him also, and I shared this with one of my peers. That peer told me she had been working with the boss for a long time and didn't think he would take it well. She told me the boss really liked me, but that if I confronted him he'd shut down. So I took her advice and I was glad I did. The boss eventually came around to where I wanted him to be. If I had confronted him, I would have screwed it up. He and I would have wound up at odds and it would have gotten me nowhere.'

Dan reflected, 'Most of the time abusive bosses don't go very far, but sometimes they do. In the case I just mentioned, this guy was brilliant. He had a brilliance that allowed him to take in a lot of information and draw a conclusion that wasn't easily seen by other people. That brilliance alone was enough to catapult him up in the company. Without the brilliance he would have gone nowhere.'[44]

---

[44] Exclusive discussion with Dan Packer, October 2008.

GETTING ORGANISED

Organising your day

According to Patrick Quinlan, 'All hours are not created equally. You might slice and dice your 120 hours based on your temperament and the prevailing needs. Some people like to work real hard for a few days, then take time off. Some people prefer working less time per day, but seven days a week. Some people have more energy at different times during the year than others. Find your own rhythm. But recognize that you also have to adapt your rhythm when you're interacting with others, or when you have to fit into project schedules or other timelines.'

Pat advises: 'You can do a sort of inventory of how you spend your time and how you feel when you spend it. How you feel about what you're doing is really important. It may be that you simply feel down at a certain time of the day, and if it just so happens you are doing the same task at that time every day, you may develop the mistaken opinion that you don't like the task, when it's really that you don't feel well at that time. At least become observant of this kind of thing. It probably varies from one individual to another, so you have to take your own inventory.'

Pat says: 'Once you get a good idea of where you're spending your day and how you feel throughout the day, you can try to organise your day in a way that minimizes wasted time. But be aware you'll always expand the work to fill the time you have.'[45]

Gilles du Chaffaut says it's important to have several things to work on in a given day. Ideally the different tasks should be of different flavours – for example, tasks requiring different levels of energy, different amounts of time, and that you enjoy to varying degrees. 'If you start out your day with several tasks in mind,' Gilles told me, 'then you work on one at a time, depending on your situation and your state of mind. Throughout the day you have different levels of energy and concentration. You are more or less available throughout the day, and you have differently sized chunks of free time to focus on something. Work on one task or another based on how you feel at the time.'

---

[45] Exclusive discussion with Patrick Quinlan, April 2008.

'That's not the same as multitasking,' Gilles carefully pointed out. 'You should only work on one thing at a time, but keep different tasks on the back burner that you can move to the front as appropriate. I also find that when I know I have different things to look at during a day, I work them over unconsciously. Don't be too strict in planning your day. You need to have several things available to work on based on what comes up throughout the day. That's what works for me.'[46]

Organising your work

Paul Orfalea started and ran Kinko's. In large part, the enormous success of his company was due to innovation.

He stays organised by keeping lists. He has his list of big things to do, and he writes down ideas as they occur so as not to lose sight of them. (Orfalea and Marsh 2007)

According to Charlice Byrd, one of the most important elements of good time management is organisational skill. That means knowing exactly where everything is and exactly what things need to be done.

'I write things down throughout the day,' the Georgia state senator told me. 'And I check my list of priorities. I keep a pad of paper next to my bed and note things I'm thinking about. No matter how you choose to organize, what's important is that you are able to find things when you need them. At the bottom of my daily list I have a task called "file things". During the day I collect things I need to file. At the end of the day I look through them and file them as appropriate. Things I don't want to keep go into what I call "file ten". That's the trash can.'[47]

Richard Branson (2004) carries a notebook wherever he goes. In it he keeps various lists: people to call, ideas, companies to set up, and key people. Every day he works through these lists.

---

[46] Exclusive discussion with Gilles du Chaffaut, November 2008.
[47] Exclusive discussion with Charlice Byrd, May 2008.

In this same notebook he also writes down notes after each phone call or meeting. He says the discipline of writing things down not only helps him remember things, but it also forces him to listen carefully to people, because he knows he's going to write down his thoughts.

Paul Orfalea did the same thing when he was running Kinko's. He carried a notebook around with him everywhere he went, and he made all sorts of lists in it. Among other things he listed personal goals, business goals, and financial goals. He prioritised all the things he had to do, and he would frequently spend time updating his lists as his goals changed. (Orfalea and Marsh 2007)

Jim Holbrook, the CEO of EMAK, advises readers to 'employ all the tools at your disposal. Use databases to avoid having to enter the same information twice. File things in an orderly manner so you can quickly retrieve them. Touch paper once. In other words, don't keep paperwork lying around. File it, throw away or handle it. Never look at it and put it back on your desk to do something with later. I also think it's important to focus on something only when you have the time to make meaningful progress. If something is haunting you and you sit down to look at it when you know you don't have time to resolve anything, you're wasting your time. On top of that, you're only building up more frustration, because it's going to continue haunting you.'[48]

---

[48] Exclusive discussion with Jim Holbrook, March 2008.

HABITS

For one week work on developing these two habits.

Habit 7: Set aside time for focused effort
Schedule time every day to work on just one thing. Follow through and use that time as planned, ignoring distractions. Whenever it's in your power, do just one thing at a time.

Habit 8: Always look for ways of doing things better and faster
Be on the lookout for things you have to do over and over again. Look for ways of getting better at them and doing them faster.

How to work on habits
Here's a reminder of the procedure. In the morning think about the day's events that will allow you to reinforce these two habits. During the day take every opportunity to make them automatic. As a visual reminder, put this book, or a copy of this page, somewhere you can see it from time to time throughout the day. In the evening take five minutes to rate yourself on a scale of 1 to 5, with 1 indicating that you did very badly on the habit and 5 indicating that you did very well. Pencil in a rating for that day on the chart below.

HABIT	DAYS						
	1	2	3	4	5	6	7
Set aside time for focused effort.							
Do things better and faster.							

EXERCISES

Here are some exercises designed to help you optimise.

i   Over the next week schedule a little time each day for focused effort.

ii Over a three-day period note everything you do that takes more than five minutes. At the end of the period put it all on paper or in a spreadsheet to get a global view.

   a   Where can you group things by context?

   b   What things can you eliminate?

   c   What can you do to fill the remaining dead time with useful activity?

iii Given your biorhythms from the second step ('Energise'), how can you best organise your day to fit your changing moods and energy levels?

iv If you are in front of your email all day reacting to every message you see immediately, you might be wasting time. Look for a more disciplined approach to using email – for example, looking at it only at certain times. Do the same with phone calls. Try to group your calls into blocks of time.

v   Think of the things you have to do on a regular basis. Over the next week, look for ways of doing these things better and faster.

8 HEAD OFF PROBLEMS EARLY

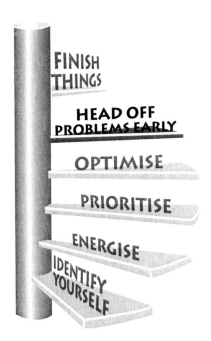

To Master The Moment you have to remain proactive and do your best to avoid getting stuck in reactive mode. This means spending time trying to predict problems that might lie ahead and preventing them from occurring. At the very least you need to spot problems early. Head them off before they develop into big messes that eat up most of your time.

Now let's turn our attention to this worthy use of your time.

CRISIS MANAGEMENT VERSUS CRISIS PREVENTION

I asked James Carter what he thought were some of the biggest time wasters. The former president of Loyola University in New Orleans didn't have to think about it. He immediately told me: 'Crisis management takes a lot more time than crisis prevention. Thinking ahead about all the things that can possibly go wrong, and trying to make sure they don't go wrong – or if they do go wrong, that they're properly contained from the beginning – that's a good use of your time. On the other hand, crisis management is not time well spent.'

Father Carter summarised: 'Being ahead of the game and foreseeing what might happen will save you a tremendous amount of time. Try to spot trouble up ahead.'[1]

Looking at the future to stay in the present

Sometimes it's hard to think about the future. There are just too many unknowns. But you can minimise your risks. It comes down to asking yourself what can go wrong and what can you do about it now.

> **TIP #32**
>
> Identify things that can go wrong, their likely causes, and actions you can take to prevent their occurrence. For each potential problem, think through what you can do if, in spite of your precautions, it does occur.

You can identify vulnerable areas and enumerate potential problems within each of these areas. For each potential problem, list the likely causes and actions you can take to prevent their occurrence. Finally, for each potential problem, list things you can do in the event that it does come to pass. The best thing you can

---

[1] Exclusive discussion with James Carter, April 2008.

do is prevent problems from arising. But they might occur anyway. So make sure you have an action plan to minimise the damage.

The CEO of Kepner-Tregoe, Andrew Graham, said: 'The funny thing is some people get so good at heading off potential problems that they forget about the dangers. Frequently you don't know what you've prevented. When it comes time to cut costs, you might tend to cut out some of the preventive measures thinking they've never prevented anything. You don't know in many cases. It's a tricky thing.'[2]

Now let's go back to my discussions with Ray Titus. The CEO of United Franchising Group told me: 'Nobody has perfect knowledge. You'll always have things you can't control. I gave up on being a control freak a long time ago. I realised you just can't control things. To a certain extent, you have to roll with what comes your way. On the other hand, I do what I can to plan for the unexpected. I look at pros and cons before I do anything. I look at the worst case scenario. I consider the curve balls that can come at me. Of course, there are some things you can't see beforehand. But in most cases there are a few early signs you can look for to spot trouble.'

Andrew Graham is CEO of Kepner-Tregoe, a consulting firm providing training and mentoring on decision making, problem analysis, and problem prevention.

Thinking about the future isn't easy. Some people throw up their hands and don't even try to look at what might be coming their way. His advice: if you take a little time to look ahead, that will be time well spent.

'Are there more things that are more important that I could be addressing?' Ray asked rhetorically. 'Definitely. But what's most important is to always aim to be on the offensive. Things will come up and you'll have to react to them. Then remember to get back on offense as soon as possible. There are a certain number of things beyond your control and you have to adjust for them as

[2] Exclusive discussion with Andrew Graham, September 2008.

they come along. Sometimes those things will prevent you from focusing on your priorities. You may not be able to help that. But know this. If you don't strive to be on offense, you definitely won't get the right things done.'

I asked Ray what he thinks is the best thing to do when the unexpected does come down. He said: 'When a crisis does occur we deal with it, and after the fact we don't spend much time second guessing. We continue to move forward. That's more of a priority and it's really a better use of our time. I don't tend to look for who made the mistake to apportion blame. One reason for that is because the person who got you into trouble is probably also the best person to get you out of it. You need that person to keep a cool head.'[3]

Remember that Master The Moment is all about being present in whatever you're doing now. One of the things that prevent people from focusing on what's in front of them is that they are anxious about the future. What we're trying to do in this fifth step is to develop habits that allow you to think about the future at specific times and in specific ways. Once you've developed confidence in this approach, you'll no longer **worry** about the future. You'll know that you've already done what you can to prepare. This frees you to stay in the present.

Biases in assessing the future

If I were to ask you to drive into town to pick up a package and bring it back, and then I asked you to put on glasses that obscured your view, you'd have a hard time carrying out the mission. The same is true for how you view problems and how you look into the future. If you can't see clearly, you can't carry out these activities.

The fact is, you can't see clearly. As a human being you have fears, prejudices, and cognitive shortcuts that skew your thinking. The best you can do is recognise ways in which your perception prevents you from seeing clearly and compensate for this.

In this section and later in the chapter we're going to get into a little more cognitive psychology. You might recognise these biases in perception and thinking, but did you know that they

---

[3] Exclusive discussion with Ray Titus, July 2008.

can be demonstrated in experiments? Daniel Kahneman and his late colleague Amos Tversky won the Nobel prize in economics in recognition of their work to demonstrate predictable ways in which we make choices in an irrational manner.

It's interesting to bring up Daniel Kahneman in a book on time management and personal effectiveness, because the story of his childhood is itself a textbook case on overcoming obstacles. A French Jew, he managed to survive Nazi-occupied France only because his family was able to stay a step ahead of the bad guys. Just six weeks after Kahneman's father died of under-treated diabetes, the Allies retook France. Kahneman was 12 at the time. Two years later his family moved to Israel. Kahneman went on to be one of the leading psychology researchers of our time. Much of his research has been around how we perceive problems and how we make decisions under risk – subjects that apply nicely to economics. Before the work carried out by Kahneman and his late colleague Amos Tversky, economic theory was based on the rational agent model, which assumes that human behaviour is completely rational. As it turns out, we are biased in all sorts of predictable ways. Some of their findings are things that many people already suspected, but Kahneman and Tversky demonstrated that they certainly do exist, and this research shed light on how natural laws operate to cause these biases. (See Kahneman and Tversky 2000; Kahneman 2002)

One source of bias is the mechanism with which we predict how we'll feel about a future occurrence. When we assess a future event we tend to focus on the transition from the present state to the future state. We think about how we'll feel during that period of change. But we don't usually take into account that we will, in fact, get used to the future state.

For example, people anticipating winning a lottery will think about becoming rich, and imagine that it will be a lasting feeling. What really happens to the few people who win the lottery is that they get used to being rich, and they settle down to approximately the same level of happiness they experienced before.

The same holds true for people planning to move to a new city. When asked about what this will do to them, they tend to assume that the feelings they have during the period of change will be extended to the whole time they're in the new city. When they actually live the event, their feelings at different points in time are quite different from what they expected.

What does this mean for time management? It means you should be aware that you are probably skewed in your thinking about the future. In order to see trouble brewing up ahead you have to find ways of compensating for these biases.

DOING IT RIGHT THE FIRST TIME

No matter what you do, if you are careful to build on solid ground you'll minimise the risk of running into trouble down the line.

Solid processes

To get really good at this, you have to set things up to run smoothly today. If all of your attention is required to react to events as they arise, or if you need to focus all of your efforts on keeping things going today, you're caught in a trap. With no time to think about the future, you can only wait for problems to rear their ugly heads – and when they do occur, they show up as urgent and unexpected events. Let's take some examples.

Twenty-two years ago, as a young software engineer, I had the opportunity to observe different management styles in the various startups I worked for in the Washington DC area. One manager, an absolute expert, could answer any question that came up concerning the application for which he was responsible. Any time there was a crisis, he jumped on it immediately. Once he figured out the source of the problem, he would explain his findings to whichever team member was available, and he would suggest a solution.

Another manager, while just as skilful as the first one, chose not to be a product expert. Rather than familiarise herself with product details, she spent most of her time building the competence of her team members. She also spent time building a good team environment and a trusting relationship between herself and each team member, and among team members.

Guess which of the two managers had time to take vacation or to get involved in broader company matters? The second one. What's more, she went much further in her career, because she spent time up front setting up things that would run without her attention. Once things ran smoothly, she could turn her attention to the future. In stark contrast, the other manager could never find the time to look at anything outside his product area.

Here's another example. I recently had the opportunity to provide a master class to a group of people starting small businesses. They all liked the parts about setting goals and prioritising. All of them were goal oriented, and ordering their activities by importance came naturally to them. But when it was time to discuss setting up solid processes, we had a lively debate. About half of them said that the most important thing is to win deals as early as possible. The other half argued for focusing first on building the capacity to do business.

The first half was exemplified by what one of the attendees said was his motto: 'Just get the deal. We'll worry about how we're going to deliver afterwards.' My answer to that was: if that's the way you operate, all you're doing is pushing off problems until they grow into disasters.

Let's look at one more example of setting things up to run smoothly. 'Process' is one of Gary Heavin's favourite words. And you can see why. He and his wife Diane started Curves and made it the fastest-growing franchise in history. Much of their success is due to the attention they placed on developing processes.

According to Gary, 'So many organisations fail to focus on the fundamentals. They just want to make the next deal and give no thought to setting up an infrastructure of principles and processes. The problem with this idea is you never go beyond the next sale.'

'Life is a process,' Gary says. 'It's not a destination. It's not some level of achievement. It's always a process. When you understand that, you can ease up on yourself.'

When you know where you want to go, plot a path to get there. If it's something you do more than once, set up a process.

Taking those same steps will help you not just that one time, but multiple times. Once you have faith in the process, you just have to think about following the steps.

The CEO of Curves applies this idea everywhere. For example, when he's looking for people who can take over certain responsibilities, there's a set of steps he goes through to accomplish that goal. Gary wants people who meet two fundamental requirements: that they can be trusted, and that they can potentially do the job as well as or better than he can. Because this is something he has to do over and over, he sets up a process that satisfies his requirements every time.

Gary says: 'Initially, I want them to watch what I'm doing in that area. I want them to simply observe. Then I go into a second phase where I watch them. The third level is where we ultimately want to be. At this level I'm comfortable with them, and I leave them alone. Once you're satisfied the competence is there, and you see they understand the culture and values, you can step back and let them do their job.'

To use this powerful idea, you need confidence in your ability to set up the right processes and in your ability to follow the steps you define. Sometimes this is counterintuitive. You're more inclined to take immediate action and solve just the problem in front of you without careful thought. While taking action, you probably tend to spend a lot of time thinking about your overall goal. This quickly becomes a major distraction, turning your attention away from what you need to do now.

If you can develop two good habits, you can make the power of process work for you. The first is the habit of slowing down to define the right steps. The other is to focus only on the step in the process you're working on at a given time.

According to Gary, 'If you have a good process, and you stick to that process, you can accomplish just about anything you can imagine. You can overcome bad habits and tragedies. You can turn your attention to the future.'

Not only will you get more done, you'll also have a better time. Gary says: 'Whether you're working on fitness, diet, or something related to work, setting up a good process allows you to relax and simply move through at a pace at which things should happen.'[4]

Preparation for the unknown

In some cases you have no idea what's up ahead. There may be too many possibilities and you just can't plan for them all. Even in these cases, you can at least prepare for the unexpected.

Illustrating this point, Suri of American Reprographics said: 'You're always going to have urgent situations. There are some things you can predict and plan for. There are other things that are beyond your control. For the ones I can predict, I do just that – I think through what could go wrong and what we are going to do about it in the event it occurs. For the ones beyond my control – when faced with such an emergency, I think of solving a class of problems, so I'll be better at dealing with that type of situation next time.'

'Even in an emergency room, you can have some control,' Suri pointed out. 'One day a guy comes in with a stab wound, the next day somebody comes in from a car accident, and the day after that somebody comes in from a gunshot wound. How do you plan for that?'

'You can't really plan,' he told me in answer to his own question. 'But you certainly can prepare. When you're working in an emergency room, you know you're going to get surprises. That's your job. When a taxi races up to the emergency entrance with one or more desperate patients, you know one thing. You know that you have no idea what's in the taxi. So you prepare yourself. You have blood ready, you have the instruments ready, you have doctors ready. You know to expect the unexpected.'[5]

I asked Patrick Quinlan about this topic. The CEO of Ochsner Health Systems told me: 'We never do predict the future very well. We simply can't anticipate the unknowns – the variables that really change things. What you can do is prepare so that you expect change. You can increase your capabilities, so that when something unexpected is upon you you're better able to deal with it.'[6]

[4] Exclusive discussion with Gary Heavin, April 2010.
[5] Exclusive discussion with K. Surivakumar (Suri), March 2008.
[6] Exclusive discussion with Patrick Quinlan, April 2008.

The 21st commandant of the US Coast Guard, Admiral James Loy knows all about being prepared.

He likes to say that preparation equals performance. If you pre-pare well, you perform well. Staying prepared is a good use of your time.[7]

What are some good ways of preparing? As city manager of Grenoble, France, Gilles du Chaffaut has some experience in this matter. He told me: 'We try to map out all the different problems that might come our way. We could have a disaster like a flood or a fire – or an act of violence, maybe a riot. For each risk we first look at how to minimise the likelihood the problem will occur. Then we look at how we can spot it in the event it does occur. Finally we scope out what we'll do if it comes to pass. We do all of this ahead of time.
One thing I've learned is that even if you've carefully planned your reaction to a problem you need to leave room for change. You never really understand what's going to happen ahead of time, so make sure you build in the flexibility for those closest to the problem at the moment it occurs to react according to what they see. Don't be too prescriptive.'

Gilles advises: 'This is what we do to run a city, but the same principles apply on a personal level. Think of every problem that might come your way. Then for each risk, think of how to avoid it, how you recognize it if it does occur, and what you can do if it does occur. That's the best you can do – and it sure is a lot better than being surprised and unprepared.'[8]

Another person who knows a lot about being prepared is James Loy. Former commandant of the US Coast Guard and former Deputy Secretary of Homeland Security, he says: 'There are so many things beyond your control that in many cases the best thing you can do is be prepared. If you prepare well you perform well. The catch phrase I like to use is "Preparation Equals Performance."'[9]

---

[7] Exclusive discussion with James Loy, May 2008.
[8] Exclusive discussion with Gilles du Chaffaut, November 2008.
[9] Exclusive discussion with James Loy, May 2008.

The laws of inevitability

As discussed earlier in this chapter, we have trouble assessing future events. We don't do a very good job of predicting how we'll feel about something months or years from now.

Aware of this bias, Steve Hansel tries to compensate when planning ahead. The former CEO of Hibernia National Bank told me: 'I find it especially important to be careful when you make decisions far ahead of time. The further out something lies in the future, the less seriously you'll take any outcome – even if you know the outcome will be painful. In other words, you'll accept just about anything, as long as it's scheduled far enough out. But these things will come to pass. When they do, you'll regret having agreed to certain things out of haste or in a moment of weakness.'[10]

In the same vein Jim Whitehurst of Red Hat says: 'You have to be careful what you say. Sometimes you'll say "yes" to something and wind up spending a week sorting out the consequences. You have to be very thoughtful about what the consequences will be, in a few months, of what you say or do now. Think about how you're going to feel in the near future when it comes back your way. Will you look back on it and consider it a good use of your time?'[11]

Ray Titus thinks that future pain or future gratification seems so far off that people aren't willing to do what it takes in the present to lay the groundwork for a better tomorrow. Ray says: '"Sacrifice" is a dirty word these days. Take, for example, what we've seen with the stock market. As we've seen recently, anything can happen. Everybody's looking for things too fast. We've promoted the idea of 22- or 23-year-old CEOs who have founded companies. That does happen, and hats off to those who are able to do this. But let's remember how rare this is. The problem is everybody thinks they're entitled to it. Therein lies the danger. People are not able to give up things in the short term for long-term gains.'

'People don't think things through,' Ray summarised. 'You need to have a goal, and you need to think about what you're willing to give up to get what you want. Not everybody accepts the idea of

---

[10] Exclusive discussion with Steve Hansel, March 2008.
[11] Exclusive discussion with Jim Whitehurst, April 2008.

giving something up. The average person today is overextended. People live for today and they're very selfish. It's all about them and today. That's a problem.'

'I like to call these phenomena "the laws of inevitability",' Ray told me. 'Some things are sure to happen. There is a determinism. Yet no matter how clear the consequences are, some people still do the wrong things.'[12]

SPOTTING TROUBLE UP AHEAD

As Chancellor of the University of Maryland, William Kirwan has 25,000 people working for him. He also has to pay attention to a number of stakeholders, including state politicians, researchers, students, and sports fans.

He spends time thinking about what might come up, and he works out a mini plan for all possible scenarios. He says: 'A very important element of time management is to leave the time necessary to go over contingencies.'[13]

Simply making a conscious effort to spot trouble up ahead is already a big step. If you're not doing so already, start taking just a little time every day to think about what might lie down the road. Progressively spend more time on this until you feel you've reached an appropriate level.

To better understand the art of spotting trouble up ahead we can also look at the practices of Herb Kelleher and other executives that made Southwest Airlines a huge success. To minimise the chances that the company would be caught off guard they would go through a process they called 'future scenario generation'. During this process strategic planners would ask a lot of 'What if?' questions to imagine future scenarios Southwest might find themselves in. For each plausible scenario they would then draw up a plan. (Freiberg and Freiberg 1997)

---

[12] Exclusive discussion with Ray Titus, July 2008.
[13] Exclusive discussion with William Kirwan, May 2008.

Todd Davis does something similar. 'I allocate time either to myself or to other executives to work on strategy against our mission,' the CEO of LifeLock said. 'How can we get to where we need to be? Where might we be vulnerable, or what might impede us? These are the questions we ask.'

'We do this on a regular basis,' he said. 'The process is simple and concise, and it doesn't take long. It simply involves stepping back and taking the view from 10,000 feet, saying "This is my mission", "Am I doing the right things to accomplish it?", and "Where are the vulnerabilities that might prevent me from carrying out my mission?", or "What can I do to bolster my position ahead of time?"'

TIP #33

The more you trust your system of looking ahead and thinking about what might occur in the future, the more you can relax and focus on the present.

Todd does this in business and he does it in his personal life. Because he thinks about the future on a regular basis, and because his approach is methodical, he has developed a confidence that allows him to spend most of his time fully focused on what he's doing now.

As we saw before, anxiety about the future is one of the things that prevent us from focusing on the present. If you have this problem, you won't be able to eliminate it overnight. But you can improve progressively.[14]

Taking the long-term view

Randy Rose advises: 'You need to develop an intuition about what's going on under the surface, or about what's lurking around the corner. If you don't develop a feel for this, you can't be effective.'

---

[14] Exclusive discussion with Todd Davis, March 2008.

Randy Rose returned to his home town of Green Bay, Wisconsin, to take on the Chief Executive role for Enzymatic Therapy in 2002. Before that he was Chief Operating Officer in Energizer Holdings.

Randy is constantly looking down the road to see not only what's next, but what's next after what's next.

He shared with me some of the practices he uses to help him think about the future. 'You may have heard the idea of always asking yourself "What's next?" Well, I have a variation on that theme: "What's next after what's next?" In my opinion, thinking like that allows all people who have a stake in where we're going to prepare themselves accordingly and to work that into their own plans. Thinking about what's next after what's next and communicating that to stakeholders has the additional advantage of making people feel involved.'

'I go so far as to write the annual report for the future,' Randy said. 'I write in the future annual report what we will have accomplished to get from wherever we are now to wherever we want to be. I also include in the report projections for the future – that is, "what's next after what's next". This sets direction and minimises fears people might have about our intentions.'[15]

Keeping an eye on what the other stakeholders want
One way to predict what's coming down the road is to stay up on what other people are thinking. Those people who have a stake in whatever it is you're doing are likely to have an opinion on your direction, whether they be business partners or family members and close friends with an interest in your personal wellbeing. If what you're doing is inconsistent with what they want, you need to be aware that this could spell trouble up ahead.

Along those lines Randy Rose advises: 'If you go forward with something without first having an idea how the other stakeholders feel, you may run into trouble later. Even if you ultimately don't agree with the other interested parties – and this will frequently

---

[15] Exclusive discussion with Randy Rose, March 2008.

be the case – let them air their ideas. Maybe they will change your opinion. If they don't, go forward with your instinct. At least you know where the other parties stand and you will have given them a chance to state their case.'

> **TIP #34**
>
> Make sure no stakeholders feel alienated, and take the time to understand their positions. These are good ways of heading off problems early.

'Walking around and talking to people helps me spot problems early,' Randy says. 'Because I invest time in engaging people in casual conversation, they tend to point out potential problems I might not see otherwise.'[16]

Manuel Esquivel, former Prime Minister of Belize, has a similar approach. He says: 'Heading off problems early comes from anticipating what might become a roadblock. You can do that by putting yourself in the other person's shoes. You might think you have a good solution, but the other person might not like it at all. You have to think about what you want to do, and what he wants, and ask yourself if you can live with what he wants. Is there a way to find a middle ground? If you anticipate what the other person will think, you can work this out ahead of time.'[17]

Seeking advice

Another way to spot trouble up ahead is to go out and talk to people who aren't necessarily stakeholders but who have experience in key areas. By making it a habit to seek their views, you create a regular flow of information that will help you spot problems early.

Somebody who puts this idea to use is Dan Packer. The former CEO of Entergy constantly looks for advice. 'There are very few

---

[16] Exclusive discussion with Randy Rose, March 2008.
[17] Exclusive discussion with Manuel Esquivel, June 2008.

situations you come across that somebody else hasn't been through,' he says. 'Ask around. Either somebody you know has words of wisdom for you, or they know somebody else who does. Occasionally you'll get into an area nobody else knows about, but that's rare.'[18]

TIP #35

By seeking advice from other people you increase the flow of information towards you. This allows you to get a better view of where you are and what lies down the road.

In working with small business owners, I can see this principle play out. Clearly some of them are out asking other people for their opinions. These are the ones who are able to quickly assess their situation and make changes as necessary. In the long run, the results reflect this.

During a Census year, as director of the US Census Bureau Louis Kincannon had half a million people working for him. During other years there are around 14,000 people in the bureau.

Louis advises taking the time to listen to what other people have to say. They can probably tell you something you didn't know before – and a positive side-effect is that a person who feels listened to is a person more motivated.[19]

Still, many people have trouble asking for advice. Pride gets in the way. It's true that you make yourself vulnerable when you ask somebody else for their opinion. They might take it as a cue to tell you what to do. Some get carried away and talk your ear off. Filtering out all the useless things in search of a nugget can be exhausting. But isn't raising the chances that you'll spot a problem early worth a few minutes of discomfort?

---

[18] Exclusive discussion with Dan Packer, October 2008.
[19] Exclusive discussion with Louis Kincannon, May 2008.

Let's finish this topic of seeking advice with a word of caution. When you go out and ask other people for their opinion on something you're doing, don't mistake this for asking permission, and don't think you have to take all advice. The ideas they have for you may or may not be appropriate. You have to weigh this yourself and make your own judgement as to which advice you want to take.

SOLVING PROBLEMS EARLY

Facing the cannons

Once you spot trouble, the best use of your time is to deal with it quickly. Face the problem head on. Lucas Skoczkowski of Redknee offers his words on this subject. 'Always face the cannons,' he says. 'If somebody shoots at you, you should always move towards them right away. If you run away from them and try to avoid them, you'll get shot in the back. I read a lot of military history, and this particular idea comes from what I've read about the US Marines. Translating this into professional and everyday life: if you see an issue, tackle it ASAP, especially if it's an issue that can grow over time. Face it, deal with it, and then move on. Otherwise, it's only going to get worse and shoot you in the back.'[20]

TIP #36

When there's a problem, go to it immediately. You will have to face it sooner or later – and sooner gives you a better chance of successfully resolving it.

When I asked Ward Klein, the CEO of Energizer Holdings, about these ideas he told me how he personally evolved in this area. 'Early in my career my initial reaction was to hesitate when faced with an uncomfortable situation,' he said. 'But over time I realized: if you don't say "no" early on to something you don't like – or if you don't face a problem head on and at an early stage – the issue will nag you. So you really have to learn to do just the opposite: confront the problem early and be honest with yourself when you're uncomfortable. Realize "I'm not comfortable with the situation."

---

[20] Exclusive discussion with Lucas Skoczkowski, April 2008.

191

Find out why. Then give it your best shot to resolve the issue. It's important not to shirk an oncoming issue. Strip out the emotion, identify the problem, and do your best to tackle it immediately.'[21]

Bias in problem solving

To do that, you need to get a grip on any fears that might prevent you from facing a problem. David Novak, CEO of Yum! Brands, has an interesting view on his own fears. His observation is that fears are usually about the future. Most of the things we fear never happen, and most of the rest don't turn out the way we expect them to. (Novak with Boswell 2007) Nevertheless, fears are real, and you can't make them disappear. With practice, however, you can recognise them for what they are and do your best to override them.

We are biased by fears and by our background, but we also have trouble seeing clearly because our brains simply can't process everything. We take cognitive shortcuts. While you can't prevent your brain from working this way, you can at least be aware that your thinking might be biased and apply reasoning to make up for it. This idea of listening to your intuition and then applying a mental tool to compensate is called 'bounded rationality.'

Jean-René Bouvier, CEO of Buzzinbees and a former vice-president at HP, compensates for some of these cognitive shortcuts by keeping an eye on orders of magnitude. 'I always keep in mind the rough orders of magnitude of various things, such as the population of a country, the revenue of a company, or the number of cell phones sold,' he says. 'Whenever I see a number, I can compare it to a number I know and I can ask myself if the number is really true.'

Jean-René says: 'I'm not interested in minute details, but I can get an idea of whether something is in the right ballpark. Words like "big" or "small" don't mean anything to me until I get a rough order-of-magnitude comparison.'[22]

---

[21] Exclusive discussion with Ward Klein, March 2008.
[22] Exclusive discussion with Jean-René Bouvier, April 2010.

HABITS

For one week work on developing these two good habits:

Habit 9: Build solid processes
Set up processes that last and that run without your attention.
Doing this will allow you to look to the future and head off
problems early. Where you have established processes, work
within them. Don't 'wing it' when you don't have to.

Habit 10: Spot trouble ahead and solve problems immediately
Set aside time to think about what lies ahead. Put in place ways
of getting regular feedback from people so that they'll help you
spot trouble. Face all problems as soon as you can.

How to work on habits
Here's a reminder of the procedure. In the morning think about
the day's events that will allow you to reinforce these two habits.
During the day take every opportunity to make them automatic.
As a visual reminder, put this book, or a copy of this page,
somewhere you can see it from time to time throughout the day.
In the evening take five minutes to rate yourself on a scale of
1 to 5, with 1 indicating that you did very badly on the habit and
5 indicating that you did very well. Pencil in a rating for that day
on the chart below.

HABIT	DAYS						
	1	2	3	4	5	6	7
Build solid processes.							
Spot trouble ahead.							

EXERCISES

Take the time to go through these exercises, designed to help you integrate the ideas from this step – to head off problems early.

i   Although it might be uncomfortable, spend a few minutes thinking about things that have gone wrong in the past, and that you could have predicted and done something to prevent – or at least to minimise the damage they caused. Make a note of these things and of why you weren't able to head them off.

ii   We tend to think of painful situations in the future as not important, almost as if we thought they wouldn't really occur. To what degree do you have this problem, and what can you do to compensate?

iii   Think of ways you can better set things up in your day-to-day life to run without your attention. Add what you come up with to your list of actions for the near future.

iv   Set aside time every day to think about the future. Put this on your top five list if it helps, or you might schedule time in your electronic calendar.

v   Think about each of the WILL DO goals you set up in the fourth chapter. Remember that the WILL DO goals are, by definition, within your control. List some of the things outside your control that might go wrong. What can you do to minimise damage should these things occur? Doing whatever you can to head off trouble, and to minimise damage once trouble occurs, is within your control.

9 FINISH THINGS

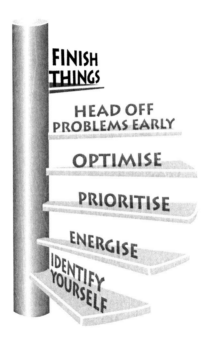

A woman who attended one of my introductory seminars told me she thought she made the most of every day, and therefore didn't really need much help in time management. A single mother, she gets her two kids off to school every morning and then drives to work, where she manages a small team of support professionals. Her team always comes out near the top in terms of metrics.

When I asked attendees to make a list of things they set out to do in the past but either didn't finish or finished much later than was appropriate, I noticed that she took more time than others. During that part of a seminar I talk about attitudes towards goals, and how different attitudes affect performance and whether you drive the task through to completion. That's where I hooked her. It turns out that she was very efficient in all that she did, but she had a hard time finishing what she started. This bad habit didn't show up in her work because her job involved reacting to problems and she never had to drive a project to completion.

This woman had a long list of unrealised goals. Earlier in her adult life, two classes short of finishing a university degree, she had decided to quit school to start a job she thought at the time was too attractive to pass up. More recently she had been through all the motions of getting a loan to purchase a house, but then got distracted by other things and never got around to buying a home. Even though she did all the right things, she didn't finish what was important.

As this case demonstrates, no matter how much effort you put into something, if you don't bring it to completion you've probably lost precious time. Crossing the finish line is a fundamental element of good time management.

Of course things do tend to change as you get into a project. The reasons you started out with may no longer be valid. You also learn more as you go along, and through this better understanding it might become clear that the project is not worth finishing. In such cases you need to do the opposite of what we just discussed. Instead of finishing, you need to cut it out. If you don't, you waste your most precious resource: time. In terms of time management, stopping what needs to be stopped is just as important as finishing what should be finished.

Usually this is not a question of judgement. More often than not it's quite clear what should be continued and what should be stopped. The challenge is more a question of emotion and attitude – having the strength of character to act on what you know you have to do. Finishing things can be difficult if you are afraid of the outcome. You may see a successful outcome as a way of demonstrating your talent; the flip side of this thinking is that you view failure as an indication that you lack some of the talents you thought you possessed. The outcome is all the more important and maybe even something to be dreaded.

Cutting your losses is at least as difficult, especially when you have to admit a degree of failure. We naturally tend to avoid any admission of failure, so it's tempting just to let things continue in hopes that somehow a turnaround will occur. It's also hard to let go of something you've started and maybe taken a liking to – consequently you have trouble giving it up. When stopping something means disappointing other people who have a stake in the project, the emotions run even higher.

Let's take a closer look.

CROSSING THE FINISH LINE

Les Hirsch received national recognition for his tenacity in keeping Touro Infirmary operating in New Orleans in the aftermath of Hurricane Katrina. Les told me: 'I can't overemphasise the importance of sticking with something and getting it done. So many people have the right ideas, get started working towards them, and may even get most of the way there. Then they lose sight of their goal and give it up before completion. What a waste of time!'[1]

Steve Hansel, former CEO of a large bank, added his ideas to the discussion. 'I always tell people that the ultimate productivity is to do it right the first time. To do it right the first time, you have to finish it.'[2]

But, according to Dan Packer, 'Everybody has trouble finishing things. I've had problems finishing things for one reason or another. I've always thought I had a reason – an external reason – but the reality is there's usually an internal reason and an external reason. You might also call the external reason a "compelling event" that forces you to make a decision you had already been working over unconsciously.'

---

[1] Exclusive discussion with Les Hirsch, March 2008.
[2] Exclusive discussion with Steve Hansel, March 2008.

TIP #37

Time spent working on something you don't bring to completion is probably time wasted.

'Take for example, the period in my life when I stopped school the first time and joined the Navy,' Dan said. 'My father just had a heart attack, and both my sister and I were in school. My sister had a scholarship, and I was on a partial scholarship. We still depended on my Dad financially. He was working three jobs and my mother was working two jobs.'

'This was in the 60s,' he continued. 'We both chose to go to private schools. My sister went to Xavier and I went to Tuskegee. It was a very tumultuous time in the United States. One semester – just after Martin Luther King got killed – we took over the campus. George Wallace's wife, Lurleen, was officially the Governor, but George was really the one running the state.'

Dan, who is African-American, explained, 'The Alabama National Guard, which was all white at the time, came on campus with tanks and personnel carriers. I can tell you that was a scary time! Somehow we finally got that all straightened out. Everybody went home, took a breather, then came back. We had been out five or six weeks. I was an engineering major. That next fall I was worried about my Dad and I thought maybe what I should do is leave school.'

Dan went on: 'The political climate was hard and my Dad had just had a heart attack. I added it all up and decided to leave. I could have added it all up and decided to stay. Other people might have done that. I'm not sure which way was right, but that's what I did. I left, joined the Navy, and got married.'

'Sometimes I think about it and say that others who were with me finished school and got their degree on time,' Dan said. 'Then again, they may not have had the family problems I had. I thought Deborah, my sister, was smarter than me. I thought it would be easier for me to go in the military. I just wanted to stay out of Vietnam.

But actually I wound up going to Vietnam. I thought my baby sister needed to stay in school. I figured the military would pay my way through school later. I had gone through that logic.'

Former CEO of Entergy, a Fortune 500 company providing energy to southern Louisiana, Dan Packer has something to say about bringing things to completion.

It's easy to make excuses for not finishing something. Usually there's an internal reason and an external reason for not completing things. While it's easy to attribute the cause to some external force when you aren't able to take something across the finish line, it's usually because you're uneasy about something. Take the time to figure out how you really feel.

Talk about follow through. After his military service Dan went to night school to get a business degree. He then worked his way up to becoming the chief operator of a nuclear power plant and then he became CEO of Entergy. That's Dan Packer's story – a very public one. Most people aren't so well known, but they can still learn from what Dan said, because the same elements are present in lives of less public figures.[3]

Given all the advantages of finishing things, why is it that some people lose sight of their goals? Why do some people get distracted and move on to something else, never coming back to what they set out to do?

Keep your eye on the goal, but not constantly
Ray Titus shared with me some of his observations. 'People have great intentions when they start with something,' he said. 'For example, they set out with the dream of buying a Corvette. They might even take a picture of one and put it on the wall. They might set up a savings account and make some sacrifices to put money aside.'

---

[3] Exclusive discussion with Dan Packer, October 2008.

'Somewhere along the line they get sidetracked and stop working towards their goal,' Ray said. 'Then one day they pull up alongside a Corvette at a light. They look over at it and ask themselves why they haven't reached their goal. The light turns green and the Corvette speeds away.'

In high school Ray Titus wrote a paper on franchising. His teacher was unimpressed and gave him a bad grade. Years later Ray became known as something of a franchising guru. CEO of United Franchise Group, in 2007 Ray was named Ernst & Young's Florida Entrepreneur of the Year and the Counselor International Person of the Year.

Ray ran into that teacher one day in Long Island and they both had a laugh. Ray advises finding some way of reminding yourself of your goals to help you stay focused when things get tough.

He explained: 'When people don't finish something it's usually one of three things. They didn't write down the goal in the first place. They didn't have a plan including how long it's going to take and what sacrifices they would have to make. Or they didn't put in place a way to help them stick to the plan. For example, they didn't put a picture in front of them to help them stay focused.'

'In most cases it's the first thing,' Ray said. 'They don't write down the goal. Then maybe only 10 per cent of those who write it down write down a reasonable plan to achieve it. Finally, of those who take the time to write down goals and make the plan, many aren't disciplined enough to find ways of staying focused. What a waste of time it is to get sidetracked after having set the goal and having put considerable effort into reaching it.'

Ray summed it up with these words of advice: 'If you get good at this process of writing down goals, putting together a plan, and staying focused on implementing the plan you can stay on the offensive. You'll get things done.'[4]

---

[4] Exclusive discussion with Ray Titus, July 2008.

TIP #38

You should keep your eye on the goal but spend most of your time thinking about what you need to do now to get to where you want to be.

While it's important to keep the goal in mind, if you start thinking more about the end state and less about what you need to do to get there, you're sure to spin your wheels. Frank Stewart advises: 'Don't celebrate success too early. The same goes for lamenting failure: don't sit around imagining you'll fail in the end. You should keep your eye on the goal, but spend most of your time thinking about what you need to do now in order to get to where you want to be.'[5]

Short tasking

When you work towards a big goal, you usually can't bring it to completion in one go. But you can break up the big goal into small tasks, each of which has a clear end. As Scott Goldman points out, 'In business as in sports or in anything else you do in life, there are benefits to gathering momentum. You can only achieve that momentum when you have focused effort, or uninterrupted time to bring something to an intermediate completion point.'[6]

The lesson here is to divide activities into chunks of time concluding in some measurable result. When you take a chunk of time to do something make sure you have a good stopping point – a plateau that will allow you to feel a sense of accomplishment, and from which you can easily pick up where you left off.

Jean-René Bouvier of Buzzinbees said: 'I divide my work into meaningful units and put them into the context of an overall plan. I try to have a view of the overall puzzle as soon as possible. Where there are missing pieces, I put placeholders to revisit when I have a better understanding. Then I attack the different pieces one by one. When you finish a unit you get a sense of accomplishment. Then you go on to the next one. Sometimes I'm not even conscious

[5] Exclusive discussion with Frank Stewart, April 2008.
[6] Exclusive discussion with Scott Goldman, March 2008.

201

of this process; other times I write it all down. Divide and conquer is a powerful concept.'[7]

Another CEO who applies what he knows about sports to other parts of life, James Ravannack, says: 'I believe in short tasking. That's what works with kids. It's worked well with my son in college, for example. An international business major, part of his studies includes learning Chinese. He found it very difficult and somewhat overwhelming. I advised him to short task. Break the problem up into components and focus on progressing one component at a time. Don't look at the problem as a whole. Doing so will at best be a distraction, and at worst it can be so intimidating you throw up your hands and walk away.'

'I personally don't believe in long-term goals,' Jim said. 'You get frustrated and you give up on them. I personally don't set goals four or five years out. I don't think that's how the world works now. You have no idea what's going to happen.'[8]

Communicating the value of what you finish

Admiral James Loy advises not only finishing things, but taking it a step further. 'Hand off things in a way that ensures the other person sees the value of what you've done. When you deliver something, put the bow on it. Give it the final touch.'[9]

What Admiral Loy says reminds me of a young software engineer who attended my training. He was very bright and usually finished his work on time. In spite of all his efforts he was getting bad performance reviews and wasn't sure why. His boss told him on numerous occasions that he wasn't producing enough, but this young engineer saw things differently. He told me he thought he was putting out a lot, and having discussed this at length I have no doubt he was right. The problem turned out to be that he gave very little attention to communicating what he finished. He thought his work was obvious and that any time spent trying to explain to others what he had accomplished was time wasted.

---

[7] Exclusive discussion with Jean-René Bouvier, April 2010.
[8] Exclusive discussion with James Ravannack, April 2009.
[9] Exclusive discussion with James Loy, May 2008.

We put a lot of effort into finding ways of communicating the value of completed work. In his case this was through short and concise written reports, along with five-minute one-on-one discussions with all of the people involved in using what he produced. This seemed to help; since he started taking the time to 'put the bow' on what he delivered, he has received much better reviews.

The lesson is: not only do you have to finish what's important, but unless you communicate the value of what you've done to those to whom you hand it off, you might have wasted your time.

PROCRASTINATION

One of the behavioural patterns that frustrates people attempting to get things done is procrastination. Even those who keep their eye on the goal sometimes put off doing what's necessary to get there. This is just another form of self-sabotage.

Procrastination might be defined as the act of delaying starting or completing tasks you consider important. Everybody procrastinates sometimes, but for some people it's a bad habit, or maladaptive behaviour. Experts estimate that as many as 20 per cent of American adults fall into this second category, that of chronic procrastinators. These are people who habitually fail to act on their intentions to perform a task. They prefer to engage in pleasant tasks in the morning, putting off unpleasant tasks to the evening. They live in perpetual frustration because they feel they can't start important projects, or they can't finish what they start.

Why we procrastinate

Why do we procrastinate? The reasons abound. Some people do it because it thrills them to do things at the last minute. They might imagine they perform better under pressure, or they simply enjoy the emotional high they get when working under pressure. While nothing conclusively contradicts the idea that some people work well under pressure, some studies have shown that chronic procrastinators turn out to perform very poorly when under the gun.

Of course cases do exist where people have demonstrated spectacular performance under pressure. But these cases rarely involve people who intentionally delay action in order to pull a rabbit out of their hat at the last minute. For example, you might have seen films and documentaries showing how well the Apollo XIII crew and NASA mission control performed under pressure. We are all impressed at how skilfully and courageously they managed to get the three crew members back safely to Earth. However, it's unlikely that anybody involved in that mission would be labelled a chronic procrastinator – one of those people who habitually put off doing something they consider important. If they were, they probably wouldn't have passed the stringent requirements to get into the space programme in the first place. Those involved in Apollo XIII didn't create their own pressure – they were under pressure due to circumstance.

Sometimes people put off doing things they perceive as unpleasant or boring. This comes as no surprise. When an alternative presents itself, most of us are tempted to give in to the distraction and set aside the less interesting task. In many cases, though, the task is perceived as unpleasant or boring because it wasn't taken on by choice, or because the outcome of the task has unwanted consequences.

People also put off doing things they feel forced into accepting. After all, nobody likes to feel enslaved. In our earlier discussion of what motivates people, we talked about the importance of feeling autonomous in choosing to perform a task. The more people feel a sense of volition in taking on work, the more they will be motivated, and they put in their best effort. Consequently when people feel that they have freely chosen to take on a task they are less likely to procrastinate. Remember that when we bring up coercion, we're not just talking about coercion from the outside. You can also be coerced to do something by internal forces. For example, if you do something out of pride, or to avoid feeling guilty, you are forcing yourself to do it. You will experience the same symptoms as if you were coerced from the outside, because here, too, you won't be taking on the project with a sense of volition. (Blunt and Pychyl 1999)

To summarise the previous points: people procrastinate for the thrill of doing something at the last minute, to avoid unpleasant or boring work, or as an act of defiance when they feel forced into doing something. But one final – and in fact, the most common – reason people tend to procrastinate is that they think the outcome of whatever it is they're doing will say something about their self-worth. Studies have shown that when two groups of people are asked to do the same task and each group has the same alternative tasks or distractions competing for their attention, if one group is made to view the task as simply a game and the other views it as a way of evaluating themselves, those in the second group are much more likely to divert their attention to the alternative tasks. In other words, the second group – the group that expects the outcome to reflect on their self-worth – will tend more towards procrastination. (Fee and Tangney 2000)

TIP #39

Most of the time people procrastinate, it's because they think the outcome of whatever it is they're doing will say something about their self-worth.

This sounds familiar. It's similar to our earlier discussion on how some people view projects as a way of evaluating their native ability, whereas others see them as something they can learn to do by working at it. For the first group, depending on the outcome, the results will serve either to praise their talents or to condemn their shortcomings. By contrast, the second group will have a more healthy attitude toward the project and will fare better in overcoming setbacks. We see from the present discussion that people in the first group are more likely to procrastinate, because they need to fend off the prospect of being evaluated upon task completion.

Research psychologist Joseph R. Ferrari says that when people procrastinate to put off being evaluated, in many cases they're handicapping themselves. If they put off working towards an outcome, they are then able to claim that poor performance was a result of a late start or lack of effort rather than a statement of their native ability. Chronic procrastinators are excessively concerned about their image, and consequently they try to avoid situations that might make them look bad. For these people, it's better to do nothing than to risk failure or risk looking foolish. According to Ferrari, you can reduce procrastination if you can view some components of the task as fun games rather than as practice leading up to a threatening evaluation. (Ferrari and Tice 2000; Scher and Ferrari 2000; Ferrari, O'Callaghan and Newbegin 2005)

How we procrastinate

People procrastinate in a number of ways. One common method of putting off doing what you should be doing is to divert your attention to something else. Lucas Skoczkowski told me what he thinks about this. 'Sometimes people take on too much work in order to set up a system of distractions,' he said. 'When you take on too much, it might be a way of avoiding doing the one or two things you really should be doing. This is a problem I've had personally, and I'm working on moving into a new phase of time management where I select one or two important tasks to focus on at a time.'[10]

Another way people procrastinate is by not making a decision. As Steve Simpson told me, 'Nothing is perfect in life. You can't sit around waiting for perfect conditions to act. A lot of times I find you have to move on something and then adjust as you go along. Nobody has perfect information in the beginning – you develop your understanding as things evolve. It really comes down to knowing yourself. You have to know when you're hesitating out of fear versus when you're hesitating out of good judgement. Then you need to muster the courage to move forward despite your fears.'[11]

Sometimes procrastination hides beneath a guise of perfectionism. Steve Hansel illustrated this point to me. 'The first time I remember being able to have an impact on this phenomenon was when I first became CFO of Barnett Banks,' he told me. 'By nature of my job, I was in charge of putting out the annual reports. When I started, we were getting them out in mid March. Up until March 10th or March 12th, people were sitting around talking about the report, and we had a highly paid lawyer looking it over, changing commas to semicolons or something like that. There was a whole lot of nitpicking going on.'

---

[10] Exclusive discussion with Lucas Skoczkowski, April 2008.
[11] Exclusive discussion with Steve Simpson, March 2008.

'So I said: "This is crazy! We aren't getting anywhere." I then set an arbitrary deadline to get this done and have it printed by February 1st. And so we did it. We got it done a month and a half early simply because we set that goal.'

Steve summarised: 'I think, you generally do what you organize to do. If you organize to get something done by February 1st, then you get it done by that date. On the other hand, if you say "We're in no hurry, we'll do it by March 15th," then you'll do it by March 15th. But you'll spend more hours, because you'll be splitting hairs. At some point the law of diminishing returns kicks in.'[12]

It's also worth noting that the reasons for procrastinating make a difference in where and how we procrastinate. As psychologist Brian Little observes, any project moves through four different stages: inception, planning, action, and termination. Depending on how you feel about what you're doing, you're likely to procrastinate at different points in the project. For example, when involved in a project lacking in pleasure or personal meaning, you tend to procrastinate during the inception, planning, and termination phases. When working on something where you feel you have little control – or where there is a high degree of uncertainty – you'll tend to procrastinate mostly during the action phase. When working on a project for which you feel a lack of volition, you're likely to procrastinate mostly during the inception, action, and termination stages. Finally, when you find an activity boring or frustrating, or when you resent the activity, you will probably procrastinate across all phases. (Little, Philips and Salmela-Aro 2006)

Procrastination in creative work

Jim Holbrook is CEO of EMAK, a publicly traded marketing services firm. He relies on new ideas in his work.

Jim points out that procrastination rears its ugly head in different ways. Sometimes you have to set work aside – for example, when you're out of ideas. Just make sure you're not putting things off out of fear.

---

[12] Exclusive discussion with Steve Hansel, March 2008.

Procrastination shows up in strange ways when you're trying to create something. Since Jim Holbrook runs a marketing services firm, I thought he'd be able to tell me something about procrastination when what you're doing is somewhat artistic. Indeed this was something he had thought a good deal about. 'When you're doing creative work, it's difficult to impossible to estimate how long something will take,' he said. 'You can't force creativity. You might sit around for hours without inspiration, and then in a matter of seconds you have a flash. Once that idea comes to you, depending on its nature you need more or less time to work through the details. The fact is, some ideas take longer to hash out than others. There's no predicting it.'

'Of course when your ego gets in the way, strange things happen,' Jim said. 'The other reason creative work is so vulnerable to procrastination is: when you come up with an idea, there's always a fear it will appear ridiculous to other people. It's highly personal. Indeed, some of your ideas will turn out to be ridiculous. There's no doubt about that. But you have to remember it's not going to destroy you, and you're not going to be ostracized for having a few weird ideas. As much as possible you have to avoid attaching your ego to what you produce. The more you can separate your own self-worth from your ideas, the more likely you'll come up with good ideas and present them to people. As counterintuitive as this might be, it's really true.'

Jim summarised: 'For these reasons, when you're doing something creative procrastination can rear its ugly head in a number of ways. The times you spend sitting around trying to come up with ideas can get rather boring, and you can easily get tempted to do something else. You might check your email or flip through papers on your desk. If you bend to that temptation and get distracted nobody will notice. But then again, the frustration will build up in you.'[13]

Letting things stew
Gilles du Chaffaut adds a counterpoint to this discussion. The city manager of Grenoble, France, says that sometimes it's appropriate to put off what you're doing. These are times when you're

---

[13] Exclusive discussion with Jim Holbrook, March 2008.

working on something you just can't do immediately. The answers aren't available to you at the time, or you just don't have the temperament to work on it. Gilles says: 'In this situation, no matter how much you want to work on the task, you do need to put it aside and let it stew. While it's stewing you tend to work on it unconsciously. As other things come up, you tend to spot new ideas that can be applied to the difficult problem you've put aside. You let your intuition work the difficult problem and sooner or later answers will come to you.'

'That's not the same thing as procrastination,' he says. 'You have procrastinators at one extreme, and on the other extreme you have people who think they need to work on the problem right away and to completion. In both cases time gets wasted. In the case of the procrastinator, things that can be finished aren't finished. At the other extreme people exhaust themselves trying to accomplish something they aren't ready to accomplish. They spin their wheels trying to do the impossible, and that's also a waste of time.'[14]

OVERCOMING FEAR AND FRUSTRATION

A lot of times we aren't able to finish what's important because we aren't able to get beyond certain fears or we get frustrated by intermediate failure and aren't able to push forward.

Your attitude concerning obstacles
For help on this, let's consider people who have had to overcome the frustration of a seemingly endless sequence of losses. As mentioned in the first chapter, John Dane III, one of the CEOs featured in this book, has been trying out for the Olympics for the last 40 years. He finally made it – at the age of 58! He has been able to motivate himself when others would fall apart. John approaches his business with the same tenacity.

'I like to win,' he said. 'Closing a $30 million or $90 million boat deal is a challenge. It may take over a year to win a deal like that, and these projects tend to simmer. When you win it feels really great. But chasing the contract and winning the deal – that's only a great start. Then, three years later I hope it's rewarding financially.'

---

[14] Exclusive discussion with Gilles du Chaffaut, November 2008.

At the age of 58 John Dane III competed in the 2008 Beijing
Olympics. He is also CEO of Trinity Yachts.

Of course John gets frustrated from time to time. But when he
loses, he does his best to learn from his mistakes. Then he gives
it another go.

'What about when you lose?' I asked. 'Don't you ever lose? And
when you do, what do you do to rebound?'

'Oh, yeah! There are tons of deals where we work really hard and,
for a variety of reasons, things just don't work out,' he acknowl-
edged. 'I just pick it up, hope I learn from it, look back and see
what mistakes I might have made. Was it the overall economy?
Was it something we did or didn't do? I try to learn from the
experience and avoid making the same mistakes again.'[15]

Here's what Les Hirsch told me about dealing with a tough
situation: 'I have been in a very stressful area – New Orleans,
post Hurricane Katrina. It's kind of like being in debt and never
getting your balance paid off. You work really hard and it never
seems to be enough.'

Les Hirsch was named hospital administrator of the year in 2005
in the United States. Hired as CEO of Trouro Infirmaries two
weeks before Katrina struck, he had to draw on years of playing
basketball on a competitive level, and years studying martial arts,
to stick to his work.

He says that quite frequently it's the person who perseveres who
wins out over the one with more ability.

'We feel very strong economic pressure to get over the hump,' Les
said. 'The costs to do business have skyrocketed beyond our control: labor costs, utility costs, property and casualty insurance

---

[15] Exclusive discussion with John Dane III, March 2008.

costs, etc. We can't turn around and raise our rates to the Government. There's usually a lag in time between our realizing the costs and the Government's raising the rates accordingly.'

Les went on to say: 'There are a lot of things beyond my control. I'm spending a disproportionate amount of my time communicating my circumstances to state and Federal Government. We're making enormous progress because we continue to provide quality health-care at our expense. But we're digging into our own funds. That's not sustainable.'

He explained: 'Leadership has many characteristics, but some of the aspects you need in this situation are tenacity, courage, and a strong sense of perseverance. The worst thing you can do is take on the role of being a victim. I want people to understand our situation and empathize with us, but I don't want them to feel sorry for us. I want them to understand our legitimate needs.'

'I don't wake up in the morning feeling frustrated – I wake up knowing I have to keep my eye on the ball,' Les said. 'You wake up knowing what your target is, and knowing you cannot lose sight of that target. Then you muster the tenacity and mental toughness to face the situation.'

He finished his thought: 'For the people around you, you have to create a sense of enthusiasm and optimism. Let people know there is hope. Don't give anybody around you an excuse to play the role of victim.'[16]

I knew Gert Boyle could tell me a lot about overcoming frustration. As you'll recall from the first chapter, she lost her husband at the age of 47 and was forced to take over the family business, a small clothing store. A homemaker with absolutely no experience in busi-ness, she managed to overcome her initial feelings of frustration to turn Columbia Sportswear into the company it is today.

She told me that she was very down during the first few months following her husband's death. But she learned early in life that you can't sit at home crying for too long. You need to react. Gert

---

[16] Exclusive discussion with Les Hirsch, March 2008.

told me: 'I know it sounds trite, and I know you've heard it before. But it's a fundamental truth we forget too easily. So I'll repeat it. How you deal with frustration makes all the difference in the world. Everybody gets knocked down. Those who succeed are the ones who fight back.'

> **TIP #40**
>
> Don't let frustration keep you down. Spend your time thinking about now and the future.

'One thing that may have helped me deal with frustration is that I was taught very early in life to put my energy into the present and the future,' Gert explained. 'It's a big waste of time to sit around feeling sorry for yourself or to torture yourself over past mistakes. That time can be better spent doing what you need to do now to make things better. While you may not see results immediately, acting in the present is much better than feeling sorry for yourself about the past.'[17]

Among his various other occupations in life, James Ravannack is president of the US Olympic Wrestling Committee. His contributions to the sport have won him a place in the Wrestling Hall of Fame. James said: 'People tend to look behind them and not forward. You see this in personal lives and you see it in the business world. The ones who are looking behind are the ones who stay where they are. It's the ones who are looking forward who succeed more.'[18]

Fear of failure / fear of success
On failure or success, Charlice Byrd told me: 'I think we put too much emphasis on the word "success", and we become too fearful of not achieving our goals exactly as we defined them. Therefore nobody wants to take on the challenge. Sometimes we set goals that are far beyond what we can possibly achieve. We then consider ourselves a failure because we haven't reached that goal. How do you overcome this kind of fear? I haven't quite figured that out yet.'

---

[17] Exclusive discussion with Gertrude Boyle, August 2008.
[18] Exclusive discussion with James Ravannack, April 2009.

'I will say this,' she continued. 'When you start second-guessing yourself on everything you do, that's when the failure comes in. When you step into the fire you know you're going to have to take a beating – the good licks and the bad licks. If you're standing up for what you believe in and everybody opposes what you represent, then you have to stick to what you believe. Be man or woman enough to fight for what you believe.'[19]

Named by *Asian Times* magazine as one of the 25 most influential Asians in Georgia, Charlice Byrd knows how to bring things to completion. As House Representative for the state of Georgia, she has had to push some tough legislature.

Charlice says that when you're doing something worthwhile, at some point somebody's going to turn on the heat. Fight for what you believe and finish what you start.

Sometimes people attach their ego to an outcome, which makes the stakes so great they can't get over intermediate failure. Again we see the idea that if you view either success or failure as a statement about you as a person, you are more likely to be crushed by setbacks. Perhaps James Ravannack sums up this idea best. 'If you lose a contract or if you gain one, it doesn't change who you are as a person,' he told me. 'Things are going to happen to you in life; some are good and some are bad. Appreciate the good things and accept the bad. Neither changes your core.'[20]

CUTTING YOUR LOSSES

The flip side of finishing things is recognising that something is no longer worth doing and then giving it up. Sometimes it becomes clear that you're working on a losing proposition, but you're so emotionally attached that you can't give it up. You may think that somehow you can recover your losses.

---

[19] Exclusive discussion with Charlice Byrd, May 2008.
[20] Exclusive discussion with James Ravannack, April 2009.

> Michael Dell emphasises the importance of recognising problems early and having the strength to cut your losses and move on to something else as quickly as possible.
>
> Be quick to recognise a losing activity, and be quick to get out of it.

Nobody can reasonably argue that Michael Dell hasn't made good use of his time. One of the things he does well is quickly get out of a losing activity. He writes in his book *Direct from Dell* that 'it's human nature to shrink in the face of bad news or disappointment, and to hope that something will just happen to make the situation better. But something magical usually doesn't happen, and the time we waste in denial is always crucial.'

He goes on to say: 'One of our sayings is "Don't perfume the pig." By that we mean "Don't try to make something appear better than it really is." Sooner or later the truth will come out, and you are better off dealing with it head on.' Sometimes this means cutting a losing activity. (Dell 1999)

Leading psychology researcher Daniel Kahneman says there is a basic human aversion towards cutting one's losses. According to Kahneman, we more easily adjust our point of reference upwards than downwards. If your stock portfolio goes up 10 per cent, you easily reset your net worth accordingly. If on the other hand your portfolio goes down by 10 per cent, it's much more difficult to adjust your reference point. (Kahneman and Tversky 2000)

TIP #41

It's much harder to adjust your point of reference downwards than it is to adjust it upwards. This is one of the reasons people have so much trouble cutting out of a losing activity. Recognising this bias will help you overcome it.

Dan Packer says the difficulty in cutting one's losses is sometimes due to what he calls 'emotional contracts' – when you have a commitment to an idea or to the people involved in an activity.

Dan told me: 'Emotional contracts are good and bad. Sometimes you want to have an emotional contract to effect some change. Other times it masks the things you need to know about a person. A lot of times you have to break an emotional contract to cut your losses. You have to look ahead and see that, as much as you love doing something, you have to stop doing it because it leads to bad things. Once you believe that, it becomes a little easier to cut a losing activity.'

Dan expanded on this: 'I use the world "believe", and I'm talking about internal attitude. Make sure you know how you truly feel about it. Of course it's hard to sit down and tell a lot of people you're going to stop doing something when they expected to keep going. There's no getting around that. But you can make the best of it by showing them respect and giving them the information you have.'

'The best you can do is try to communicate how you came to the decision to cut out,' Dan continued. 'Now, that's very important – but it's not something everybody does well. You can be dead right on your decision to stop a losing activity, but if you don't communicate the rationale behind that decision, you're going to upset a lot of people. You have to trust that people will be mature enough to accept tough facts if they understand the reasons behind it and if they trust the person communicating those reasons.'

He reminded me: 'We talked about this in the context of delegating. It's the same thing. You have to learn to do that communication well. That's a habit worth developing. When it comes time to communicate tough decisions to people, it helps a great deal if you have laid a groundwork of trust beforehand. If over the years you've shown you're somebody who tells it like it is, you'll have that foundation to work from.'[21]

The sooner you cut your losses, the quicker you can move on to what you need to be doing. If you don't let go, you worsen the loss.

If your bigger plan is a good one, you can make decisions to bail out of the smaller things that aren't working along the way. You're

---

[21] Exclusive discussion with Dan Packer, October 2008.

not going to win on everything, so don't be afraid to give up some battles. Just make sure you win on the big things and make sure you stick to the big plan.

When cutting your losses means admitting you made a mistake, consider what serial entrepreneur, Nick Mueller, says. He relates, 'I've probably learned more from the smaller failings than from things that do work. You don't really know for sure why you succeed in every case, but you usually know, when you fail at something, why you failed.'[22]

Let's complete this thought with what Gary Heavin says on this subject. The CEO of Curves puts it this way: 'If you stick with the rule of never making the same mistake twice, pretty soon you'll run out of mistakes.'[23]

CRUMBS

Bringing something to completion is good to do for the task at hand, and it also has some nice side-effects. Patrick Quinlan shared his thoughts with me. 'I find that what really drives people crazy is when they can't see the end of their work – when they can't anticipate a good outcome. Finishing things and achieving satisfaction from the results fuels you for the next task. You also build confidence in yourself by delivering on a promise you made to yourself to complete the task.'[24]

Remember you have very limited capacity. But you can work within natural laws to make the best use of what you have. Instead of viewing a large overwhelming goal, break it up into meaningful units of work. Each chunk of work should be something you can complete in a reasonable amount of time and it should represent a building block towards the overall goal. We'll call these CRUMBs, as an easy reference. They are:

---

[22] Exclusive discussion with Gordon Mueller, April 2009.
[23] Exclusive discussion with Gary Heavin, April 2010.
[24] Exclusive discussion with Patrick Quinlan, April 2008.

Clearly

Realisable

Units

that serve as

Meaningful

Building blocks

Each crumb should take a quantity of time and resources that allows you to build up success. It's important to aim for just the right amount of work – something you can certainly complete, but that is at the same time challenging. After you complete one you should gain in satisfaction, which provides you extra juice to propel you through the next crumb. This creates an upward spiral in which finishing one thing gives you a positive reward, and helps you complete the next crumb better and faster.

Because a crumb represents a 'meaningful building block', when you are not working on that particular crumb you can think of it as a whole, and forget about the details – about what's inside. In some cases your crumbs won't be such that you can complete one before going on to the next. If you are building a business your crumbs will be ongoing processes, such as generating leads or turning leads into clients.

In other cases your crumbs will be arranged in a series. For example, if you're working towards a university degree, you can take each class as a crumb. Or you can even break up a course in to smaller crumbs to focus on just one aspect of what you have to learn at a time. Don't think about all the challenging classes you have to take next year. Think only about the chunk of work in front of you now.

In all cases your crumbs should be units of focused effort – while you are working on a crumb, you only need to think of that crumb. Frustration in one crumb should not spill into another. I can't overemphasise the importance of mentally compartmentalising so that you only have to think about one thing at a time. You achieve the right state of mind while you are doing the work, and you can gain a sense of accomplishment each time you finish a crumb.

David Smétanine, a tetraplegic as a result of a 1995 car accident, went on to win medals for swimming in the Paralympics (one bronze in 2004; two gold and two silver in 2008). He is also an elected official in France.

David says: 'I spend most of my time thinking about working on technique and doing my best during training sessions. You need to cut up your big goals into small things that are easy to carry out. Taken together, the small things will allow you to accomplish the large, difficult goal.'[25]

To give you another example, a marketing specialist I coached told me she never felt satisfied. Most people were surprised to hear this. Anybody looking from the outside would think she was very competent and that she accomplished more than most people. But her frustration was real.

I had her break up all her goals into crumbs and then schedule work on each crumb. I also had her schedule time just to play, with absolutely no end in mind. Her problem was she was thinking of all things at all times. We put together a virtuous cycle where the more she separated activities in ways that allowed her to think only about what she was doing in the present, the more she would feel a sense of completion. The more she trusted this process of cutting things up and the more she trusted herself to get done whatever was in front of her, the more she was able to achieve a state of relaxed concentration.

Let's further illustrate the idea of crumbs with two hypothetical examples.

---

[25] Exclusive discussion with David Smétanine, April 2010.

Getting a job – example of using crumbs
You need to find streams of information on available jobs. This includes two separate activities: reading what's publicly available and working your network. You need to build up your pitch. This consists of a good CV or résumé, good references, and interview techniques. You need to target different job categories and alter your pitch accordingly. You need to approach companies. When you get an offer, you need to negotiate a contract. Each of these activities is a separate crumb. There's no need to mix your attitude about negotiating a contract with your state of mind when you are building up your pitch.

If you have trouble approaching companies, or if you get turned down a lot, you'll feel frustrated. By working with separate crumbs you can prevent that frustration from spilling over into the other crumbs associated with your goal. Doing so will allow you to put 100 per cent into the task at hand.

Starting a company – example of using crumbs
You need to develop partnerships based on trust. You need to develop a legal structure. You need to find clients. You need to develop your products. You need to develop procedures. Each of these is a crumb.

Developing a legal structure is something for which there is a clear end date. On the other hand, finding clients is not. You can divide that crumb into even smaller chunks, such as finding the initial clients or developing procedures for finding clients. That way you can achieve a sense of accomplishment and measure your progress.

HABITS

For one week work on developing these two good habits.

Habit 11: Break your goals into small units of work, and think only about one unit at a time

Periodically review your goals, and when you do, break them up into meaningful building blocks (crumbs). Spend most of your time working on one crumb at a time. Think only about the one you're working on, and avoiding spending time dreaming about the big goal.

Habit 12: Finish what's important and stop doing what's no longer worthwhile

Finish things you think are important. And remember, finishing means communicating the value of what you've done. For things that no longer make sense, cut your losses as early and gracefully as possible.

How to work on habits

Here's a reminder of the procedure. In the morning think about the day's events that will allow you to reinforce these two habits. During the day take every opportunity to make them automatic. As a visual reminder, put this book, or a copy of this page, some-where you can see it from time to time throughout the day. In the evening take five minutes to rate yourself on a scale of 1 to 5, with 1 indicating that you did very badly on the habit and 5 indicating that you did very well. Pencil in a rating for that day on the chart below.

HABIT	DAYS						
	1	2	3	4	5	6	7
Break goals into small units.							
Finish what's important.							

EXERCISES

Here are some exercises designed to help you finish what's important and stop doing what's not worth completing.

i   Make a list of things you've finished but for which you could have done a better job communicating the value of your work. Now write down what you could have done to 'put the bow' on what you delivered.

ii Make a list of cases where you didn't get out of a losing activity. Spend time thinking about why you weren't able to get out. Were you too attached to the activity? Did you have trouble accepting the fact that you took a loss? Was it too hard to tell other people you were stopping?

iii For each of your WILL DO goals define a set of CRUMBs.

iv Review what you're doing regarding WILL DO goals. What do you need to continue and what do you need to cut? How about your WILL DO goal itself? Is it still worthwhile?

v   Try the following tomorrow. Don't spend any time thinking about long-term goals. Just think about what you have to do right now.

PART III:
YOUR NEXT STEPS

10 PERSONAL CHANGE

At the end of each of the preceding six chapters I provided two habits to work on. The intent is to get you used to working through this process to start turning the ideas in this book into reflex. Concentrate on two habits per week over a six-week period and then start again. Repeat this cycle several times.

It's likely you'll miss a day or two here and there. When this happens, don't give up. Just keep going through the six-week cycle. This is a good way to start. It helps you get used to the ideas and gets you started on a disciplined approach. Once you get the hang of it, you'll be ready to move on to something more rigorous.

MAXIMISING PROGRESS

Working on two habits a week is a good way of getting used to the process. **But focusing on a single habit a week will allow you to make bigger changes.** The daily work is similar to what we've already done. Spend five minutes in the morning thinking about the new behaviour. Carry around a visual reminder, such as a copy of the rating questions in the Appendix. At every opportunity during the day, try to reinforce the new habit. At the end of the day, take another five minutes to rate yourself.

How you rate yourself will be different now. Instead of giving yourself an overall rating, let's get more precise. In the Appendix I've provided four component behaviours for each habit. For each component give yourself a rating from 1 through 5 as you did before.

You might modify the components I've provided. If you don't like the ones I use, try coming up with some of your own. The point is to get more specific in how you score yourself now that you're working on one habit at a time.

There are two benefits to rating yourself. The first is that it forces you to think about what you did during that day. The second is that it provides you a way of measuring progress over time. If you maintain a consistent scheme, you're sure to notice an improvement in the score.

Once you get used to working on the twelve habits one at a time, **you can then work on a single habit a month,** working through the cycle in a year. That might sound like a long time, but remember that time management is something you can always improve. This process provides you a framework for development.

ASSORTED TIPS

Let's finish with a few more tips from the CEOs featured in this book.

Define your mission

Todd Davis advises: 'You need to take time to define your mission. There are people running around who don't know what their mission is. I don't know how anyone can manage their time under those conditions, because they don't even know what's important. Here's a case where you need to slow down to go faster. Slow down to define your core values.'

'This holds for individuals and for corporations,' Todd says. 'For example, here at LifeLock we have one single core value: do as you should, not as you can. This allows anybody in the company faced with a decision on how to respond to something to go ahead and make a decision based on that value system and know that even if the decision was a mistake they will get the support of the company, because they can back up that they thought they were doing what they should and not what they could. People become more effective because you can be quick in deciding and you know you will get support. You don't have everybody second-guessing you.'[1]

---

[1] Exclusive discussion with Todd Davis, March 2008.

Thierry Grange, who's in charge of the Ecole Supérieur de Management in Grenoble, France, says it's important to align your mission with the world around you. You shouldn't try to fight against nature, and you should try to make use of what's already in place. 'I don't try to reinvent the world,' he told me. 'I align myself with the way things work, and I work towards objectives that are consistent with the world around me.'[2]

Patrick Quinlan is CEO of Ochsner Health Systems, which with 10,000 employees is Louisiana's largest private employer.

He advises taking the time to understand your mission in life. Once you do that, priorities fall out naturally, and then you know what you have to do every day.[3]

James White, who runs Jamba Juice, told me that having a mission is a good way of giving yourself direction, and it's also necessary when you're giving somebody else direction. You have to lead yourself first, and then you can lead others. But to do either you have to have a mission.

James puts it this way: 'It's important to have a clear vision of where you're going. This allows two things to happen. First, you can set goals and prioritize based on your mission. Doing that allows you to apply resources to deliver the results. Second, you can provide leadership and direction.'[4]

Ray Titus said: 'We tell people: dreams are goals that were never written down. If you don't write them down, they remain a dream. If you write them down, they become a goal. And you have to strategize and plan to make that goal happen. You have to have goals. You have to want to accomplish something over a period of time.'

'If you don't communicate where you want to go and what you want to do, you're not going to get there,' Ray told me. 'If you tell

---

[2] Exclusive discussion with Thierry Grange, April 2008.
[3] Exclusive discussion with Patrick Quinlan, April 2008.
[4] Exclusive discussion with James White, April 2008.

no one, you won't get help. If you tell five people, you might get three or four people who will help you. The more people you let know what you want to do, the more chances you have of getting help. If I can get more people helping me to accomplish my goals, it takes me less time. This leaves me more time for my family, more time for my health, and more time for my hobbies.'[5]

On this subject, James Carter observed: 'It sounds obvious, but not everybody really sits down and thinks about where they're trying to go. It takes some discipline – and you can't be a perfectionist, because you frequently won't have a clear picture right away. But even without perfect vision you can decide on a direction and leave room to refine that as you learn more. It's okay to start out with a general sense of where you're going and home in on a more specific target along the way.'

Completing this thought, Father Carter said: 'As somebody once said, "You can get there real quick if you don't know where you're going."'[6]

Always learn

Mark Radtke runs Integrys Energy Services, a Wisconsin-based energy company with $10 billion in revenue.

Mark relies on his daily top five list. He may not get everything done by the end of the day, but the list keeps him focused on the important things. One thing he considers important is to learn something new every day.

Gert Boyle advises: 'Try to do better every day. If you can't do better today, then do better tomorrow. That's the way I've always seen it, and that kind of thinking has served me well. I put my energy into the present and the future.'[7]

---

[5] Exclusive discussion with Ray Titus, July 2008.
[6] Exclusive discussion with James Carter, April 2008.
[7] Exclusive discussion with Getrude Boyle, August 2008.

Mark Radtke says: 'Learn a little every day.'[8] And James White relates: 'I keep myself in a constant mindset of learning. That is critically important individually and when leading an organization. The one place where I invest daily is in my learning.'[9]

Lucas Skockowski says: 'When I interview people for jobs, I ask them how many books they read a year. On average, people read a very small number of books a year. The number one reason they give for not reading is: "I don't have time."'[10]

Ray Kroc wrote in his autobiography: 'When you're green you grow; when you are ripe, you are about to rot.' (Kroc with Anderson 1977)

Similarly, Richard Branson (2004) says he is very inquisitive. He is always asking questions and trying to learn new things. How else would he have been able to go from running a magazine for students to running a string of record stores, and then to running a record company, an airline, a soft drinks company, and so forth? On top of that he's involved in extreme sports like ballooning around the world. I think it's fair to say that Richard Branson is interested in learning new things.

Paul Oreffice, former CEO of Dow Chemical, says it's important to allow yourself to say 'I don't know'. It's only then that you can go out and learn what it is you don't know. (Oreffice with Hanlon 2006)

Nick Mueller said: 'It's been my observation that the most success-ful people are those who tend to go out and learn on their own what they need to know. They read books, they go to seminars, and they seek advice from experts. They do whatever it takes to learn.'

'Sometimes you learn because you take some risks and you chal-lenge your abilities,' he said. 'But you shouldn't be taking foolish risks – they should be calculated. And you should work out a way of getting out of trouble ahead of time. For example, you might identify a set of people who can come in and help you out

---

[8] Exclusive discussion with Mark Radtke, April 2008.
[9] Exclusive discussion with James White, April 2008.
[10] Exclusive discussion with Lucas Skoczkowski, April 2008.

if necessary. This pressures you to learn more. You also end up getting people smarter than you involved, which is another way to increase your ability.'

Nick said: 'Remember that you can listen a lot faster than you can talk. Use that fact. Listen to people around you, especially if you trust their judgement, their experience, and their skills. That's always been very helpful to me.'[11]

Face your fears
Lucas Skoczkowski said: 'I believe you have to face your fears – face the things you don't like. Subconsciously we all try to avoid these things. So I make a list of these things for myself, and I make facing them a high-priority task. Because it's high priority, I consult that list every day.'[12]

Turn things down
Suri told me: 'Think of these difficult tasks, such as saying "no" or not promising too much, as practice. Remember you're solving a class of problems – not just the problem at hand. Tomorrow will bring new problems. If you practice today, there's a good chance you'll have a template for dealing with tomorrow's problems.'[13]

As Randy Rose advises, 'Learn to say "no" in a way that's firm but polite. And don't worry about it after that. It's no longer your problem. If you sit around agonizing about all the things you've turned down, you'll be wasting an awful lot of time. Recognize that you have every right to say "no", and that the person you say "no" to has to respect that right. Being able to turn things down is one of your most fundamental rights as a human being. Don't be afraid to exercise that right.'[14]

Think about time management every day
You shouldn't think of good time management as a fixed point that you can reach and know you've reached it. It's a lifelong learning process: no matter how good you are at it, there's always something

[11] Exclusive discussion with Gordon Mueller, April 2009.
[12] Exclusive discussion with Lucas Skoczkowski, April 2008.
[13] Exclusive discussion with K. Surivakumar (Suri), March 2008.
[14] Exclusive discussion with Randy Rose, March 2008.

you can fine tune. In fact, every one of the CEOs I talked to for this book said they're still looking for ways to get better at time management – they think every day about how they manage their time, and they try to find ways of making improvements.

President of Tulane University for over 10 years, Scott Cowen also serves on the boards of directors of several large organisations and he has written four books.

Managing a university with a budget of almost $1 billion is much more work than managing a company with that kind of revenue. Running a university like Tulane means that you have to be the manager of several sports teams, you have to direct academics, you have to be a fundraiser, and a whole lot more. Scott says he learns something new about time management every day.

Take, for example, Scott Cowen, who told me: 'I've been president of Tulane University for a long time, and I'm still learning every day how I can be more effective – how I can make better use of my time. Have I set the right priorities? Have I set aside enough time to work on my highest priorities? What else can I do to get the most out of my time?'

'In the final analysis, time is the scarcest and most important resource you have,' Scott said. 'How you use that time will ultimately determine your personal success and the success of your organization.'[15]

Daniel Doimo agrees. He says: 'I think about time management throughout the day. I'm constantly evaluating what works and what doesn't. I ask myself over and over what I can do to improve the way I go about choosing priorities. What can I do to get better at focusing on what I'm doing? Am I good enough at turning away the things I shouldn't be doing?'[16]

---

[15] Exclusive discussion with Scott Cowen, March 2008.
[16] Exclusive discussion with Daniel Doimo, March 2008.

Lucas Skoczkowski puts it this way: 'I'm not sure I am very good at time management. Maybe what's true is that I am an apprentice who refuses to fail.'[17]

I couldn't disagree more with the first part of what he says. Lucas is great at time management! But the second thing he says comforts me. Lucas, who gets all those things done, considers himself an apprentice – just like me! I take that to mean he has a really good attitude. Despite the fact that he's already very effective, he takes it upon himself to continue learning.

> **TIP #42**
>
> Learn something about time management every day. Become a meta thinker: think about how you think and about how you act. Do so with the intention of making improvements.

Indeed, getting good at time management is work in progress. But don't take my word for it. Listen to what the CEO of American Reprographics, K. Surivakumar (Suri) has to say: 'As CEO of a fast-growing company, the demands on your time are constantly increasing. I have to take care of day-to-day tasks, but at the same time drive energy and excitement into the company. That's what a CEO has to do, especially to survive in a challenging marketplace.'

'I think about time management constantly,' he said. 'It's not something I just think about from time to time, when there's a particular problem, or when I'm frustrated. I think about it all the time. I think about being as effective as I can given the time I have. If I didn't do this, I could not do my job. I could not maintain my family life.'

Suri told me: 'Time management is one of my pet subjects.'[18]

You know what to do now.

---

[17] Exclusive discussion with Lucas Skoczkowski, April 2008.
[18] Exclusive discussion with K. Surivakumar (Suri), March 2008.

APPENDIX:
RATING PROGRESS ON HABITS

In this appendix I provide a worksheet for each of the 12 habits. Use these when you are ready to work on one habit per week. When you are ready to go to one per month, you can just copy the worksheet so that you'll have enough of them.

I've divided each of the behaviours into four components. This allows you to rate yourself with more detail.

Just as you did before, every morning think about the day's events that will allow you to reinforce the new behaviour. During the day take every opportunity to make it automatic. As a visual reminder, put this book, or a copy of the appropriate habit page, somewhere you can see it from time to time throughout the day. In the evening take five minutes to rate yourself on a scale of 1 to 5, with 1 indicating that you did very badly on the habit and 5 indicating that you did very well. Pencil in ratings for that day in the worksheet.

If you skip a day here and there, just jump back in. The important thing is to get into the process. Make it a habit to work on good habits.

HABIT 1: STRIVE TO BE AUTHENTIC

How did I do?	DAYS						
	1	2	3	4	5	6	7
Doing things for their intrinsic value, not out of guilt, pride, vengeance, etc.							
Doing what I judge important, not what somebody else judges important							
Doing constructive things and avoiding self-destructive behaviour							
Leaving my ego out of decisions, and not doing things just to be a hero							

Striving to be authentic means being as honest with yourself as you can about what you want and why you do what you do. This doesn't mean you get to do everything you want to do. You'll always have obligations. Authenticity means being honest with yourself about your motivations.

At the end of each day, for each of the four component behaviours rate yourself on a scale of 1 to 5 for that day:

1 – very badly

2 – badly

3 – satisfactory, but no more

4 – well

5 – very well

HABIT 2: FAVOUR TRUSTING RELATIONSHIPS

How did I do?	DAYS						
	1	2	3	4	5	6	7
Passing over opportunities to further a non-trusting relationship							
Jumping on opportunities to further a trusting relationship							
Being trustworthy							
Being reliable							

You'll always have to deal with people you can't trust or people you know you can't count on, but you shouldn't put much energy into strengthening your relationships with these people. Instead put your efforts into building relationships with people you can trust and count on. Make sure those same people can trust and count on you.

At the end of each day, for each of the four component behaviours rate yourself on a scale of 1 to 5 for that day:

1 – very badly

2 – badly

3 – satisfactory, but no more

4 – well

5 – very well

HABIT 3: MAINTAIN A LIFESTYLE THAT WILL GIVE YOU MAXIMUM ENERGY

How did I do?	DAYS						
	1	2	3	4	5	6	7
Exercising regularly							
Avoiding foods and beverages that bring me down							
Getting enough sleep							
Spending time just having fun							

This habit means doing aerobic exercise at least three times a week for an hour each session, eating a light lunch, and getting enough sleep. For some people this is a tall order, but remember that Master The Moment consists of steps to work on and progress in an ongoing manner. If you're starting from zero, develop this habit slowly.

At the end of each day, for each of the four component behaviours rate yourself on a scale of 1 to 5 for that day:

1 – very badly

2 – badly

3 – satisfactory, but no more

4 – well

5 – very well

HABIT 4: LISTEN TO YOUR BIORHYTHMS AND ORGANISE YOUR DAY ACCORDINGLY

How did I do?	DAYS						
	1	2	3	4	5	6	7
Tuning in to my biorhythms							
Planning my day in accordance with my biorhythms							
Looking for ways to extend moments of high energy and optimism							
Accepting periods of down time							

Make it a habit to listen to your biorhythms always, and, based on what you learn, make adjustments to the way you plan to spend your time. If you're more creative in the morning, schedule creative activities for the morning; if you're more sociable in the afternoon, schedule relationship-building activities for the afternoon.

At the end of each day, for each of the four component behaviours rate yourself on a scale of 1 to 5 for that day:

1 – very badly

2 – badly

3 – satisfactory, but no more

4 – well

5 – very well

HABIT 5: SET VERY FEW PRIORITIES AND STICK TO THEM

How did I do?	DAYS						
	1	2	3	4	5	6	7
Setting very few priorities							
Staying focused on my priorities							
Planning resources as appropriate to work on priorities							
Avoiding being seduced by lower-priority tasks							

Select a maximum of two things that are your highest priority. Plan time to work on them, making sure the necessary resources are available when you need them. Be especially careful when those necessary resources are other people who have their own schedules.

At the end of each day, for each of the four component behaviours rate yourself on a scale of 1 to 5 for that day:

1 – very badly

2 – badly

3 – satisfactory, but no more

4 – well

5 – very well

HABIT 6: TURN DOWN THINGS THAT ARE INCONSISTENT WITH YOUR PRIORITIES

How did I do?	DAYS						
	1	2	3	4	5	6	7
Accepting the fact that I can't do everything							
Resolving to say 'no' to things I don't consider important							
Saying 'no' in as clear and tactful a manner as possible							
Detaching myself emotionally after turning something down							

Get used to the fact that there are many things you can't do. Learn to detach yourself quickly from things you decide not to do. Get good at saying 'no' to other people, and do so frequently.

At the end of each day, for each of the four component behaviours rate yourself on a scale of 1 to 5 for that day:

1 – very badly

2 – badly

3 – satisfactory, but no more

4 – well

5 – very well

HABIT 7: SET ASIDE TIME FOR FOCUSED EFFORT

How did I do?	DAYS						
	1	2	3	4	5	6	7
Scheduling time for focused effort							
Using the time scheduled for focused effort							
Minimising distraction							
Doing one thing at a time when it's in my power to do so							

Schedule time every day to work on just one thing. Follow through and use that time as planned, ignoring distractions. Whenever it's in your power, do just one thing at a time.

At the end of each day, for each of the four component behaviours rate yourself on a scale of 1 to 5 for that day:

1 – very badly

2 – badly

3 – satisfactory, but no more

4 – well

5 – very well

HABIT 8: ALWAYS LOOK FOR WAYS OF DOING THINGS BETTER AND FASTER

How did I do?	DAYS						
	1	2	3	4	5	6	7
Learning to do things better and faster							
Grouping tasks by context – for example, doing all email in one sitting							
Eliminating wasted time							
Making use of dead time							

Be on the lookout for things you have to do over and over again. Look for ways of getting better at them and doing them faster.

At the end of each day, for each of the four component behaviours rate yourself on a scale of 1 to 5 for that day:

1 – very badly

2 – badly

3 – satisfactory, but no more

4 – well

5 – very well

HABIT 9: BUILD SOLID PROCESSES

How did I do?	DAYS						
	1	2	3	4	5	6	7
Building processes where appropriate							
Putting together solid processes							
Working within processes							
Doing things right the first time							

Set up processes that last and that run without your attention. Doing this will allow you to look to the future and head off problems early. Where you have established processes, work within them. Don't 'wing it' when you don't have to.

At the end of each day, for each of the four component behaviours rate yourself on a scale of 1 to 5 for that day:

1 – very badly

2 – badly

3 – satisfactory, but no more

4 – well

5 – very well

HABIT 10: SPOT TROUBLE AHEAD AND SOLVE PROBLEMS IMMEDIATELY

How did I do?	DAYS						
	1	2	3	4	5	6	7
Looking for ways of spotting trouble up ahead							
Seeking advice							
Keeping stakeholders in the loop							
Facing problems immediately							

Set aside time to think about what lies ahead. Put in place ways of getting regular feedback from people so that they'll help you spot trouble. Face all problems as soon as you can.

At the end of each day, for each of the four component behaviours rate yourself on a scale of 1 to 5 for that day:

1 – very badly

2 – badly

3 – satisfactory, but no more

4 – well

5 – very well

HABIT 11: BREAK YOUR GOALS INTO SMALL UNITS OF WORK, AND THINK ONLY ABOUT ONE UNIT AT A TIME

How did I do?	DAYS						
	1	2	3	4	5	6	7
Breaking work into small chunks							
Avoiding daydreaming about the outcome							
Reaching intermediate stopping points							
Compartmentalising, so that frustration in one CRUMB doesn't spill into another							

Periodically review your goals, and, when you do, break them up into meaningful building blocks (CRUMBs). Spend most of your time working on one crumb at a time. Think only about the one you're working on, and avoiding spending time dreaming about the big goal.

At the end of each day, for each of the four component behaviours rate yourself on a scale of 1 to 5 for that day:

1 – very badly

2 – badly

3 – satisfactory, but no more

4 – well

5 – very well

HABIT 12: FINISH WHAT'S IMPORTANT AND STOP DOING WHAT'S NO LONGER WORTHWHILE

How did I do?	DAYS						
	1	2	3	4	5	6	7
Finishing what I consider important							
Communicating the value of what I finish							
Doing things on time							
Cutting out activities that are no longer worthwhile							

Finish things you think are important. And remember, finishing means communicating the value of what you've done. For things that no longer make sense, cut your losses as early and gracefully as possible.

At the end of each day, for each of the four component behaviours rate yourself on a scale of 1 to 5 for that day:

1 – very badly

2 – badly

3 – satisfactory, but no more

4 – well

5 – very well

REFERENCES

Baumeister, R.F., Vohs, K.D. and Tice, D.M. (2007), The Strength Model of Self-Control. *Current Directions in Psychological Science*, 16, No 6, 351–355.

Biswas-Diener, R. and Diener, E. (2001) Making the best of a bad situation: Satisfaction in the slums of Calcutta. *Social Indicators Research*, 55, 329–352.

Blunt, A.K. and Pychyl, T.A. (1999) Task aversiveness and procrastination: a multi-dimensional approach to task aversiveness across stages of personal projects. *Personality and Individual Differences*, 28 (2000) 153–167.

Boyle, G. with Tymchuk, K. (2007) *One Tough Mother*. Carroll & Graf Publishers.

Branson, R. (2004) *Losing My Virginity: How I've Survived, Had Fun, and Made a Fortune Doing Business My Way*. Three Rivers Press.

Branson, R. (2007) *Life at 30,000 feet: Richard Branson on TED.com*. www.ted.com, 9 October.

Brenner, L., Koehler, D., & Tversky, A. (1996) On the Evaluation of One-sided Evidence. *Journal of Behavioral Decision Making*, 9, 59–70.

Deci, E.L. with Flaste, R. (1995) *Why We Do What We Do: Understanding Self-Motivation*. Penguin Books.

Dell, M. with Fredman, C. (1999) *Direct from DELL: Strategies That Revolutionized an Industry*. Harper Business.

Dement, W. and Vaughan, C. (1999) *The Promise of Sleep*. Dell Publishing.

Dweck, C. (2006) *Mindset: The New Psychology of Success*. Random House.

Epstein, L. (2007) *The Harvard Medical School Guide to a Good Night's Sleep*. McGraw-Hill.

Fee, R.L. and Tangney, J.P. (2000) Procrastionation: A Means of Avoiding Shame or Guilt? *Journal of Social Behavior and Personality*, 15, 5, 167–184.

Ferrari, J.R., O'Callaghan, J. and Newbegin, I. (2005) Prevalence of Procrastination in the United States, United Kingdom, and Australia: Arousal and Avoidance Delays Among Adults. *North American Journal of Psychology*, 7, 1, 1–6.

Ferrari, J.R. and Tice, D.M. (2000) Procrastination as a Self-Handicap for Men and Women: A Task-Avoidance Strategy in a Laboratory Setting. *Journal of Research in Personality* 34, 73–83.

Fortune (2005) 75th Anniversary Special, First in a Series: The best advice I ever got, March 21.

Franklin, B. (1993) *Autobiography and Other Writings*. Oxford University Press, Oxford.

Freiberg, K. and Freiberg, J. (1997) *Nuts!: Southwest Airlines' Crazy Recipe for Business and Personal Success*. Broadway Books.

Gerhart, K. A., Koziol-McLain, J., Lowenstein S.R., and White-neck, G. G. (1994). Quality of life following spinal cord injury: Knowledge and attitudes of emergency care providers. *Annals of Emergency Medicine*, 23 807–812.

Graybiel, A. (2005) The basal ganglia: learning new tricks and loving it. *Current Opinion in Neurobiology*, 15, 638–644.

Guth, R.A. (2005) In Secret Hideaway, Bill Gates Ponders Microsoft's Future. *The Wall Street Journal*, 28 March.

Iacocca, L. with Novak, W. (1984) *Iacocca: An Autobiography*. Bantam Books.

James, W. (1899) *Talks to Teachers on Psychology and to Students on Some of Life's Ideals*. Henry Holt and Company, New York.

Kahneman, D. (2002) *Daniel Kahneman – Autobiography*. http://nobelprize.org

Kahneman, D. and Tversky, A. (2000) *Choices, Values, and Frames*. Cambridge University Press, Cambridge.

Kepner, C.H. and Tregoe, B.B. (1981) *The New Rational Manager*. Princeton Research Press.

Klinger, E. (2008) Daydreaming and Fantasizing: Thought Flow and Motivation. In Markman, K., Klein, W. and Suhr, J. (eds) *Handbook of Imagination and Mental Simulation*. Psychology Press.

Klinger, E., Barta, S. G., and Maxeiner, M. E. (1980) Motivational Correlates of Thought Content Frequency and Commitment. *Journal of Personality and Social Psychology*, 39, 6, 1222–1237.

Kroc, R. with Anderson, R. (1977) *Grinding It Out: The Making of McDonald's*. St Martin's Paperbacks.

Kurtzig, S. with Parker, T. (1994) *CEO: Building a $400 Million Company from the Ground Up*. Harvard Business School Press.

Little, B.R., Philips, S.D. and Salmela-Aro, K. (2006) *Personal Project Pursuit: Goals, Action, and Human Flourishing*. Lawrence Erlbaum Associates.

Marcus, B. and Blank, A., with Andelman, B. (1999) *The Home Depot: Built from Scratch*. Times Business.

Miller, G.A. (1956) The Magical Number Seven, Plus or Minus Two: Some Limits on our Capacity for Processing Information. *Psychological Review*, 63, 81–97.

Myers, D. (1993) *The Pursuit of Happiness: Discovering the Pathway to Fulfillment, Well-Being, and Enduring Personal Joy.* Harper Paperbacks.

Novak, D. with Boswell, J. (2007) *The Education of an Accidental CEO: Lessons Learned from the Trailer Park to the Corner Office.* Crown Business.

Orfalea, P. as told to Marsh, A. (2007) *Copy This!: How I Turned Dislexia, ADHD, and 100 Square Feet into a Company called Kinko's.* Workman Publishing.

Oreffice, P. with Hanlon, T. (2006) *Only in America.* Stroud & Hall.

Pollock, M.L., Gaesser, G.A., Butcher, J.D., Després, J.-P., Dishman, R.K., Frankli, B.A., Garber, C.E. (1998) The Recommended Quantity and Quality of Exercise for Developing and Maintaining Cardiorespiratory and Muscular Fitness and Flexibility in Healthy Adults. *Medicine & Science in Sports & Exercise*, 30, No 6 (June) (Position Stand for the American College of Sports Medicine).

Rankinen, T. and Bouchard, C. (2002) Dose-Response Issues Concerning the Relations Between Regular Physical Activity and Health. *President's Council on Physical Fitness and Sports Research Digest*, September, Series 3, No. 18.

Saeed S., Antonacci, D. and Bloch, R. (2010) Exercise, Yoga, and Meditation for Depressive and Anxiety Disorders. American Family Physician (April 15), 81 8.

Scher, S.J. and Ferrari, J.R. (2000) The Recall of Completed and Noncompleted Tasks Through Daily Logs to Measure Procrastination. *Journal of Social Behavior and Personality*, 15, 5, 255–265.

Walton, S. with Huey, J. (1992) *Sam Walton: Made in America.* Bantam Books

Wilson, T.D., Houston, C.E., Etling, K.M., and Brekke, N. (1996) A new look at anchoring effects: Basic anchoring and its antecedents. *Journal of Experimental Psychology: General*, 125, 387–402.

Winnicott, D.W. (2005) *Playing and Reality*. Routledge Classic.

INDEX

251